Introducing Books to Children

Introducing Books to Children

by Aidan Chambers

*Second edition,
completely revised and expanded*

THE HORN BOOK, INC. · BOSTON
1983

Library of Congress Cataloging in Publication Data

Chambers, Aidan.
   Introducing books to children.

   Includes bibliographical references and index.
   1. Children — Books and reading.   I. Title.
Z1037.C442   1983   028.5   82-21357

ISBN 0-87675-284-9
ISBN 0-87675-285-7 (pbk.)

Printed in the United States of America

CONTENTS

Preface to the Second Edition

This book has been written for teachers, librarians — especially beginners in those professions — and for anyone who is concerned about how to help children grow into avid, willing, enthusiastic readers of literature. It is an attempt to take a straightforward and practical look at ideas, methods, and varying approaches which bring books and young people into contact.

This second edition has been fully revised; and I have taken the opportunity to reorganize the contents and to introduce new material about criticism and the handling of children's responses to what they read, especially through talk about books. Teaching literature is the work of a specialist; as George Sampson remarked years ago in his brilliant little book *English for the English,* "The plain fact is that every teacher cannot deal with literature and we must not expect every teacher to deal with it." But every teacher, and every librarian, parent, anyone who cares about children and literature, can and should play a part in encouraging the young to read voraciously. That is what this book is primarily about.

A few things I would ask be kept in mind throughout. A slight matter first: these days it is necessary to assure some people that when one uses "he" as a pronoun in place of "the child" so beloved of all who utter on educational matters, one of course means to include girls as well as boys. I have great sympathy with those who object to the dominance of male gender in writing of this kind, but until we have invented a pronoun that has simplicity and elegance to replace the he/she ones, I have decided to use he and she as the text required. What I will not do is depersonalize "the child" by turning him-or-her into it.

Rather more serious and difficult is the problem of ages and stages: the ages when children might best be introduced to particular books by particular methods, and the stages of the educational system — preschool, nursery, kindergarten, elementary, etc. — that can best make use of this or that approach. Much of what I have to say applies to all ages and stages, but nevertheless I have tried not to tie down my remarks too specifically in this regard. Teaching is an art not a science and those who practice it will rightly prefer to decide for themselves which of my suggestions have anything to offer the children for whom they work. My only plea is for a whole view to be taken.

I am indebted to many people in the writing of this book: scores of teachers in Britain and the U.S.A. who have helped me by sharing their experience and knowledge; my editors, who have been a constant source of encouragement; my wife, whose comments are always worth attention; and above all, the children with whom I have worked over the past twenty-five years. I must also thank the other writers who have allowed me to quote their words in the pages that follow.

Aidan Chambers
South Woodchester, June 1982.

PART ONE

Why Literature?

I

Why Bother?

To explain why I attach so much importance to beginning a basically practical book with the questions: *Why bother? Why bother so much about children's reading? Why bother about the methods of introducing books to children?* let me relate an autobiographical note, however embarrassing it may be. In a jumble of old papers I recently came across the photograph of a young man striding through a classroom door, a pile of books under his arm and an eager look in his eyes. From the way his left shoulder is tipped forward, from the set of his head and the length of his stride, one gets the feeling that he is a fully clothed sprinter just leaving the starting blocks. The young man is, of course, myself snapped twenty-five years or so ago by a cheeky thirteen-year-old during the first few months of my first teaching job. When I see that photograph now, I smile, but the young man doesn't seem to have any connection with myself.

He does, however, remind me of the way I went about my business in those early days of my teaching career; and I mention him here because his experiences parallel, I think, those of many young teachers in their first few months at work. I remember, to begin with, that the eager young man enjoyed himself greatly, and for the most part so did the people he taught. But I know now he had not a clue about what he was doing. He had vague ideas — which at the time he thought very clear ideas — and his teacher training had been helpful, stimulating even, and informative enough. But when he got into the classroom he quickly discovered that neither his ideas nor his training were much help when it actually came to doing a full day's work every school day, every school week for a school year.

Faith and arrogance got that eager young man through his first full-time months. The faith was pretty blind and the arrogance, luckily, borne with uncomplaining good humor by his colleagues. From the beginning he spent a lot of time and energy trying to get his pupils to read literature. The books included not only texts prescribed by the curriculum — texts he sometimes loathed as much as the children they were inflicted upon loathed them — but also a wide selection of books chosen mostly because he had liked them himself in adolescence, or because he felt his pupils ought at least to have tasted them.

Both his selection and his methods of introducing the books were guided more by intuition than by thoughtful planning. It was all a somewhat hit-and-miss affair. If there was a philosophy underlying what he did, it was simplistic. Reading books, he believed, was important (he could not have said precisely why) and so it was his job as a teacher of English to encourage his pupils to read. The best way to do that was to let his own genuine enthusiasm show, and by energy, amusement, pure force of personality, to draw his pupils into enjoying books first of all with him and then on their own.

To some extent this worked — haphazardly perhaps, but in a cheerful atmosphere that, though he did not realize it then, glossed over the inadequacies of his approach. It is very easy for a teacher to think he is succeeding just because his pupils are lively and laughing. Only as his experience grew did this young man see that what he did was littered as much, if not more, with failure as it was crowned with success of a lasting kind. That is, his pupils might very well have been enjoying themselves, but he was not necessarily educating them into life-long literary readers. When he realized this he came to a stop and asked himself what he was doing and why.

At first, analyzing the way he went about his work eroded his confidence, threw him off balance, dimmed some of his energetic spirit. No one likes to admit that he has been wrong, or, at best, inadequate. But that pain passed as the understanding dawned that what you think and the way you think profoundly influence what you do and the way you do it. Intuition is all very well, a few bright ideas are useful, an entertaining approach, and a charming personality put to work with energy are strong assets. But they are not enough. What one needs above all is a coherent set of attitudes, a conscious understanding of the function and value of what one is doing and teaching.

We need answers to these double-edged questions of why bother about children's books and the method of introducing books to children because, unless we are clear about the answers, we are likely to make a number of gross mistakes in trying to bring children and books together in a tensile and lasting connection. To make sure why we believe it important to bring up children as willing, avid, responsive readers of literature we have to take a step back and sort out why literature is important to ourselves.

In taking this step back we lay bare our own attitudes to literature and reading and the place they hold in our lives — attitudes which will inevitably color whatever methods we employ in our work with young people, and which are influential in more ways than the effect they have on our teaching methods. Because of all the forces at work on children, attracting them to and repelling them from literature, the attitude of adults they meet frequently — which means parents and teachers more than any others — wields an effect surpassed only by the attitude of a child's intimate peers. The stance adopted by these adults towards literature is assumed by children (whether consciously or not doesn't matter) to be the stance taken up by society as a whole.

Reading is hard work, much harder work than experienced adult readers remember, for to them the hard work has become a pleasure, part of all they enjoy in reading, as a sportsman enjoys the physical effort and the practice of technical skills involved in playing a game. If a child detects that no very strong value is placed on reading and literature by the adults around him — especially during the early stages of learning to read for himself — then he feels no compulsion to develop his own reading skill beyond the minimal, functional level we all need simply to carry on our daily lives in our print-dominated society.

This is why there is such a marked relationship between children who quickly and permanently grow into avid literary readers and a home-and-school environment where books are thought important, are frequently used, often discussed, and are everywhere in evidence. I say home-and-school deliberately. For too long we imagined that schools could do the job on their own, and indeed they have achieved great things. But we know now that the best and most lasting success in making literary readers comes when the home is right-minded about the worth of books and reading, too. We have, in fact, at last come to recognize and act on the understanding that any child who comes to school at five years old without certain kinds of literary experience is a deprived child in whose growth there are deficiencies already difficult to make good.

Those experiences will be discussed later. For the moment I just want to note that this home-and-school setting is not necessarily a matter of socioeconomic background; it is not a matter of class or money, as is sometimes suggested. There are homes-and-schools in financially poor areas where books come in for the same everyday attention as they do in some more affluent areas. Equally there are better-off neighborhoods where the prevailing attitude to literature is so philistine and ignorant that both children and adults are virtually illiterate. They can decipher words on a page with the best of them, but they rarely read for more than everyday, functional reasons or out of professional duty. Readers are not made by moneyed privilege only, thank goodness, or there would be little hope for most of us.

So what is it that is to be valued in literary reading? Why do we attach the central, overriding importance to it that we — or some of us at any rate — do? These are tricky, complicated questions. In preparing this book I made a list of the answers I most frequently came across. Here is my list.

Reading literature:
helps extend a child's experience and knowledge of life;
helps a child's personal growth — you discover yourself in literature and therefore learn to understand more about yourself;
helps a child learn to spell, and to use the mother tongue with more facility;

entertains by passing the time pleasurably and in a socially acceptable way (a child who reads a lot is often said to be a "good" child because while he is reading he doesn't "get into trouble");

helps a child's spiritual development;

teaches a child how — and how not — to behave;

stretches the imagination;

challenges and changes us;

gets us into the closest possible contact with another person — the author;

allows us to experience all kinds of human possibilities, from murder to childbirth, without suffering the consequences of undergoing the experiences in real life;

is a game-playing activity in which we "try out" various possible solutions to life-problems and see how they might be worked out before having to tackle them in reality.

Any and all these answers to the question *Why literature?* might be true. They might also be peripheral, secondary reasons that miss the main mark, the one reason that stands above all. Whatever the answer is we can be certain that it will not be simple or easy to state briefly, because it is also true that reading literature is one of the most complicated activities in which we can engage.

For me, the value of literature has never been better explored than in a brief essay by Richard Hoggart in an article called "Why I Value Literature." In it he brings together most of the fundamental ideas we need to remember as we sort out the practicalities of bringing children and literature together. So the best thing to do, it seems to me, is to study Professor Hogart's essay before going any further.

WHY I VALUE LITERATURE
by Richard Hoggart

I value literature because of the way — the peculiar way — in which it explores, re-creates and seeks for the meanings in human experience; because it explores the diversity, complexity and strangeness of that experience (of individual men or of men in groups or of men in relation to the natural world); because it re-creates the texture of that experience; and because it pursues its explorations with a disinterested passion (not wooing nor apologizing nor bullying). I value literature because in it men look at life with all the vulnerability, honesty, and penetration they can command . . . and dramatize their insights by means of a unique relationship with language and form.

"Exploring human experience" is a useful phrase, but not quite sufficient. It is too active. "Contemplating" or "celebrating" human experience might be better for a beginning, to indicate the preoccupied passivity before life in which the imagination often starts its work. And "exploring" can sound too much like wandering for its own sake, as though literature simply opens up successive territories of human response. "Searching" or even "ordering" would be better, so long as we didn't imply by either of them an "irritable reaching after fact and reason." Every writer — not necessarily in an obvious sense nor necessarily consciously, and whether in a tragic or comic or in any other manner — means what he says. Sometimes he will deny that there is a meaning. "I only wanted to write an interesting tale," he will say, ignoring that the interest of a story almost always comes from seeing the human will in action — against chaos or against order. Sometimes the meaning he intends will not be the work's achieved meaning. The ebb and flow of imaginative power within the work may reveal attitudes hidden from the writer himself. But there will be a meaning, a kind of order — expressed or implied. Whether he knows it or not, the writer will be testing the validity of certain ways of seeing life; he will be offering, no matter how provisionally, a way of ordering the flux of experience. By his choice and arrangement of materials, by the temper of his treatment of them, a writer is implicitly saying: this is one way in which we can face experience or succumb to it or seek to alter it or try to ignore it.

The attention good literature pays to life is both loving and detached. It frames experience and, in a sense, distances it. But it always assumes the importance, the worthwhileness, of human experience even when — as in tragedy — it finds much in that experience evil. So, if a writer is imaginatively gifted, his work helps to define and assert that importance, to bring experience up fresh before us. This is not a way of saying that a good writer makes an evil experience good. But his exploration is good, since it defines more clearly the nature of the evil we suffer and perform. It helps to make us believe more in the freely willing nature of man; and it helps us to feel more sharply the difficulties and limits of that freedom. Good literature insists on "the mass and majesty" of the world — on its concreteness and sensuous reality, and on its meanings beyond "thisness." It insists on the importance of the inner, the distinctive and individual, life of man, while much else in our activities and in our make-up — fear, ambition, fatigue, laziness — tries to make that life generalized and typecast.

Not all writing acts in this way. Roughly, we can say there are two kinds of literature: conventional literature and live literature. Conventional literature usually (though it may sometimes do better than its author knows) reinforces existing assumptions, accepted ways of looking at the world. Properly read, live literature — even the quietest or most light-hearted — may be disturbing, may subvert our view of life.

"Properly read" is the key-phrase in that last sentence. I said at the beginning that literature explores, re-creates and orders human experience in a *unique* way. Other activities of the human mind explore human experience, and some re-create it, and some seek to order it. One can think of philosophers or theologians or of composers or painters. I am not concerned to set literature against any of those. Literature can be discursive in the way that some philosophy is; it has, like painting and music but unlike most philosophy, an imaginative architecture. Its peculiarity is its special relationship with, its special form of engagement with, language . . . a relationship which is intellectual and emotional at the same time and is almost always a relationship by values. Ruskin said, "Tell me what you like and I'll tell you what you are." We could just as easily say, "Tell me what language you use and I will tell you what you are." Language is not simply a range of conventional signs, increasing and altering so as to express the complexity of experience; the business of grappling with the complexity of experience, with the life by time and the life by values, is itself partly carried on through and within language.

Literature can never be aesthetically pure or abstractly contemplative. There can be no such thing as "abstract literature" as there is abstract painting. By its nature — because its medium, language, is used by almost everybody in all sorts of everyday situations; and because it tries both to say and to be — literature is an art which invites impurities.

It is the most creaturely of the arts. No other art makes us feel so much that the experience must have been just like that, that desire and will and thought would all have been caught up with those gestures, those smells, those sounds. It's not reality; it's a mirroring; but it mirrors more nearly than any other imaginative activity the *whole* sense of an experience.

Literature is both in time and outside time. It is in time because it works best when it creates a sense of a certain time and place and of particular persons, when it works through and re-creates identifiable life and manners . . . Tom Jones hiding in a particular copse with Molly Seagrim, Marvell lying in a certain garden, Dimitri Karamazov in *that* prison cell, Will and Anna Brangwen in *that* cottage bedroom.

It is outside time in two ways. First, in a sense we are all used to: that, if it is rooted in time and place and is imaginatively penetrating, it will go beyond particular time and place and speak about our common humanity, will become — as we used to say more readily — universal.

Literature goes beyond time in a more subtle sense. To describe discursively, fully to paraphrase, all that an imaginatively successful scene in fiction or drama or a poem says, means and is — to do this would take an impossibly long time and would be futile. It is of the essence of the scene's or the poem's meaning that all its elements simultaneously coexist, do their work at the same time . . . so that we feel them all at once as we would in heightened moments of life, if we were sufficiently sensitive. The resources of language and form then work together to produce the peculiarly literary achievement, full of simultaneous meanings . . . Yeats writing "the salmon-falls, the mackerel-crowded seas," Cordelia replying "No cause, no cause," Margaret Wilcox crying, "Not any more of this! You shall see the connection if it kills you, Henry!," Sophia looking down on Gerald Scales's body after all those years of desertion. One could not, even at six-volume length, "write out the meaning" of any one of these; in separating the elements by space and time we would destroy the meaning.

To respond to these meanings is not necessarily easy. It is not sensible to expect a work of any depth to yield all its meanings on a first reading by almost anyone in almost any mood. Literature is "for delight," it is true — delight in recognition, in exploration and in ordering, in the sense of increased apprehension, of new and unsuspected relationships, and in aesthetic achievement. But beyond a fairly simple level (for example, rhythmic incantation) we have to work more and attend better if we want the best rewards, here as in any other activity.

It follows that wide hospitality is good. Nor need it be the enemy of good judgment. The fact that some people use their claim to being hospitable as an excuse for refusing to make distinctions is another matter; catholicity is not promiscuity. Almost every writer with imaginative ability (that is, with some capacity, no matter how intermittent or partial, to explore aspects of experience through language), almost every such writer will have some insights to give if we read him disinterestedly, with a "willing suspension of disbelief."

Such a man may in general, or in particular things, be immature or irresponsible; we may think his statements or assumptions about human life untrue or perverse. If we do feel any of these things we should say so, as exactly and strongly as we think necessary. But we ought to be clear what we are attacking. Otherwise we may dismiss a man with some imaginative ability, but whose outlook we find antipathetic, and will claim we are judging his literary powers; or we may come to believe that we find imaginative insight in a writer whose views fit our own but who is without creative ability. If we do not "entertain as a possibility" the outlook of a writer while we are reading him we shall not know what his outlook is, and will attack or praise a caricature of it.

"To entertain as a possibility" is not the best form of words but it is hard to find a better. It does not mean "to accept," because the process is more subtle than that. It means to exercise intellectual and emotional openness and charity. It means to be able to see for a while how someone can have such an outlook and to know what it feels like to have it, what the world looks like from that angle. To do this is not to "surrender." All the time, though not necessarily consciously, we are testing that outlook against life as we think we know it ourselves. With certain writers we will be all the time in a sharp double state . . . of entertaining and rejecting at once; but even then there are likely to be moments when light is thrown on a part of human experience, and some attitude which we had pushed out of the field of our consciousness will prove to have more power than we had wanted to think.

In my experience, this is likely to be true of all but two kinds of literary effort. It is not true of work which, though full of "right instincts" and intelligent technicalities, shows no effective literary imagination. Think, for example, of many of the thematic novels about moral conflict published during the past twenty years. Worse, is the bodilessly aesthetic production which tries to treat words and forms as ends in themselves. I believe that literature is certainly in one sense "play" — grave and absorbed play. But these are pointless arabesques. They do not explore, and their patterns neither mean nor mirror.

I do not think a trivial outlook will produce great literature. It may produce odd incidental insights; but, overall, a shallow view of life will produce a shallow penetration into experience. But I agree also with R. P. Blackmur who noted that we could learn something from second- and third-rate work, so long as we supplied our own irony towards it. You salt it yourself.

The effects of literature cannot be simply described — the moral effects, that is. I do not think these effects are direct, or our experience would be a simpler matter than it is. Good readers might then be good people, and good writers better human beings even than their good readers. In speaking about the moral impact of art we are not talking about a more complicated form of those ethically improving tales for children, most of which are irrelevant to the way imaginative literature actually works. Obviously, we can learn morally even if evil appears to triumph. "Moral impact" does not mean a direct ethical prompting but the effect literature may have on the temper with which we face experience.

But first, and as we have seen, literature does seek to articulate something of the "mass and majesty" of experience. Most of us (and most of our societies) are constantly tending to narrow our focus, to ignore embarrassing qualifications and complexities, to make much of the rest of the world and all experience with which we are not comfortable — to make all this into merely a backcloth to the stage on which our egos do act comfortably. Literature can help to bring us up short, to stop the molds from setting firm. It habitually seeks to break the two-dimensional frame of fixed "being" which we just as habitually try to put round others, to make us see them again as three-dimensional people in a constant state of "becoming." Literature can have only a formal use for utterly damned souls — or for saints.

It is all the time implicitly inviting us to remain responsive and alert and to extend our humanity; we do not talk quite so easily about "all farm laborers" or even about "all Russians" after we have read Hardy or Turgenev. It is implicitly inviting us to widen and deepen our knowledge of ourselves and of our relations with others, to realize that life is more this — and more that — than we had been willing to think (Emma at Box Hill, Queequeg looking down into the whale-nursery).

All this, we have to remember, may be achieved — may sometimes only be achieved — in a mythic and parabolic way. When we speak of the "moral intelligence of art" we are not speaking only of the will in action but also of a world outside the will, of the unconscious psychic life of men. It is almost impossible not to sound pretentious here; but literature — along with the other arts, which have their own ways of informing the imagination — can help us to rediscover awe.

What is true of individuals is true also of societies. A society without a literature has that much less chance of embodying within its temper and so within its organizations something of the fullness of human experience. We only know certain things by articulating them or bodying them out. This does not mean that we have to "argue them out." We may know some things only by approaching them metaphorically, as dramatic "play."

So literature can make us sense more adequately the fullness, the weight, the interrelations and the demands of human experience — and the possibilities for order. It can make us feel all this, but not necessarily act on it. We can see and do otherwise, always. But we are not then acting quite so much out of blindness or inarticulateness; we are selfishly or fearfully or willfully trying to short-circuit what we know underneath to be more nearly the true state of things. Works of literature, properly read, give us the opportunity to extend our imaginative grasp of human experience; if we *will* to act well thereafter we may be able to do so with greater flexibility and insight. In this special sense literature can be morally educative. It can guide the moral will in so far as its illuminations depreciate certain modes of conduct and, conversely, reinforce others. But it cannot direct the moral will. In so far as it embodies moral intelligence and psychic insight it may *inform* the moral will, be "the soul of all (our) moral being."

The relation of literature to "the moral will" is not simple. Literature is "a criticism of life" which must itself be judged. But we can only understand that criticism and make our own judgment on it if we first — in a sense — suspend the will, if we attend to the literature as itself, as if it were an autonomous object, and let it work in its own way. It may then be in an active relationship with our sense of ourselves, with our sense of life in time and life by values. Like the other arts, literature is involved with ends beyond itself. Things can never be quite the same again after we have read — really read — a good book.*

*Richard Hoggart, "Why I Value Literature," *About Literature*, vol. 2 of *Speaking to Each Other* (London: Chatto and Windus, 1970/New York: Oxford University Press, 1970) pp. 11-18.

II

Children, Language, and Literature

We need to expand what Richard Hoggart says in directions important to our theme.

But before setting out it must be clear what I mean by literature, a word that has come to mean many things. There is, for example, the literature given by travel agents to people who inquire about vacations, and the literature prescribed by teachers as suitable for young people to study; or there is literature in the collective, bibliographic sense, meaning all that has been written on a topic no matter what its nature or purpose.

As I am using the word here I mean:

> ... any kind of composition in prose or verse which has for its purpose not the communication of fact but the telling of a story (either wholly invented or given new life through invention) or the giving of pleasure through some use of the inventive imagination in the employment.*

I have borrowed this useful clarification from Professor David Daiches's *Critical Approaches to Literature*. It is not of course a critical definition but simply an attempt to work out some limits — limits that would enclose Peanuts and Superman as well as *Where the Wild Things Are* and *Fungus the Bogeyman*; which accommodate the work of Enid Blyton and Franklin W. Dixon (one of the pen names of the prolific Harriet Stratemeyer Adams, author of the *Hardy Boys* and other series), as well as of Philippa Pearce and Paula Fox; within which will be found lyrics of ballads, pop, and rock music as well as Wordsworth's *Prelude*, and graffiti as well as James Joyce's *Ulysses*. Criticism can come later. For the

*David Daiches, *Critical Approaches to Literature* (Englewood Cliffs, N. J.: Prentice Hall, 1956) pp. 4-5.

moment all we need say is that quite obviously works of literature admitted by such a description will differ in the extent to which they match up to Professor Hoggart's statement of value, just as different readers find greater or lesser satisfactions in books they have read.

The outcome of critical assessments of specific books is not relevant at this point in our discussion. What we are doing here is to examine the value of literature as a whole in relation to children as readers.

LANGUAGE AND FORM

Hoggart's key phrase, "explores, re-creates and seeks for meanings," brings us at once into an understanding of the value of literature for children. You would have to go a long way to find a better description of the essential vocation of childhood than that it is a time when people explore, re-create and seek for meanings in human experience with a greater intensity than at any other period in their lives. Children are occupied thus every day in their natural, instinctive play. Sound educational practice formalizes and directs play, trying to make children aware of what they discover at a speed and to a degree that, without adult aid — without "education" — would take much longer to come by, even if the same degree of knowledge and awareness was ever reached at all. Clearly, any form of human expression which has at its heart this same purpose, and helps people continue in it beyond their childhood years, must be brought into the center not only of school education but of everyone's life outside and beyond school.

Literature, if we accept what Hoggart and many others say, has such a purpose. But it is not alone in this. Music, the manual arts, genuine scientific inquiry (as against technology, which is not truth-seeking) all in one way or another explore and seek for meanings. What these others do not share between them or with literature is literature's particular attribute, a "unique relationship with language and form." So the place of language needs closer examination, which will directly lead us to an examination of form.

Ranking among the dafter exercises sometimes imposed on children is the one that requires them to describe a screwdriver or a vase or the desks they sit at, or any familiar object. They are being asked to perform what C. S. Lewis called "an eccentric *tour de force*," for language is "the worst tool in the world for communicating knowledge of complex three-dimensional shapes." Coleridge had already noted the result of such hapless pedagogy: "all is so dutchified by the most minute touches that the reader asks why words and not painting were used."

The stupidity of such classroom grind is usually obvious to the children forced into it, if not to their teachers. "Imagine," these dominies tend to begin, "that a man from outer space has come to earth. Describe a screwdriver to him as clearly as you can." The space man, poor fellow, has presumably wandered up and somehow indicated that his UFO has conked out and can you help him please? In a flash, without a moment wasted on intelligent astonishment, the poor accosted earthling gives a detailed description of the instrument he apparently assumes without further investigation the stranded space man needs. Apart from all the other curious oddities in the teacher's imagined situation, the problem of language, on which the exchange rests, is not allowed to obtrude into the exercise. Teacher is happy in the knowledge that he is teaching his pupils how to write descriptive English. In fact, all he is doing by forming the exercise in this fashion is to teach a misuse, not to say a misunderstanding, of language.

This is a large and difficult question and we can hardly do more here than crudely touch it on the nerve. In the following passage from his book *Language and Learning* James Britton pinpoints precisely what I am trying to get at.

> The cutting into segments of the stream of sense experience and the recognition of similarities between segments enables us to build up a representation, let us say, of an object such as a cup. From the overlap of many experiences, focused upon as the word "cup" is used by other people or ourselves, the basis of similarity and dissimilarity becomes more clearly defined and more objects, different from the original cup in what does not matter but alike

in what does — what defines the category — are admitted to the category. The word, then, unlike the visual image I have of a cup I have seen and can recall, is a generalized representation, classifying as it represents.

Taking a leap from there, it is difficult to imagine how some experiences could be classified at all were it not for the agency of language. Four-year-old children will cheerfully and confidently talk about their *holidays* — about who is on holiday and where they have gone, and about what they are going to do on their own holidays. The definition of the category, criteria by which to decide what is properly called "a holiday" and what is not, would be a complicated task for us and certainly the four-year-old could not attempt it. And there is nothing to point to, as he might point to a cup to show he knew the meaning. The ability to operate the category has grown from the overlap of experiences of the word *in* use as applied to his own familiar experiences.*

Words are symbols; their power lies not in themselves but in what they name and stand for and all the circumstances surrounding our experience in coming to understand them. Children need to reach an appreciation of this, just as they need to appreciate that words and what they stand for tend to become one in our minds, so that we sometimes only have to speak a word to witness a reaction in other people that should logically follow only if the object itself were present. As when "Spider!" is bellowed at someone who does not exactly care for arachnids. Words are powerful, forming and motivating our behavior. In this sense, language is magic.

When we come to deal with our imaginings, our thoughts, emotions, past and present experiences, in an attempt to sort them out, the power of language is indispensable. Until we have forged these experiences into words we are not sure what we think, feel, know. "How can I know what I think till I hear what I say?" the poet Auden reports an old woman telling him, echoing a universal realization. Most people can find no meaning, no order in their lives, cannot even recognize their existence until they have formed their perceptions into words or found them reflected in someone else's words.

*James Britton, *Language and Learning* (London: Allen Lane, 1970) paperback ed. pp. 26-27.

True of adults, this is even more affectively true of children, who cannot yet comprehend in abstract terms. They experience so much that is new and unknown to them every day — a flood tide of sensual receptions, emotions, events, ideas, data of all kinds. Much work in education is an attempt to help children learn how to articulate this confusion of experiences and so come to grips with it. Without language, the basic and demotic tool, no one would have a chance; we would go bumping around in the dark, and eventually take leave of our senses under the welter of the incomprehensible, withdrawing, as some people do, into a closed world in order to protect ourselves against the unbearable onslaught.

James Moffett, in his valuable book *Teaching the Universe of Discourse* in which he describes ways of helping children articulate their experiences, puts it this way:

> Whereas adults differentiate their thought into specialized kinds of discourse such as narrative, generalization and theory, children must for a long time make narrative do for all. They utter themselves almost entirely through stories — real or invented — and they apprehend what others say through story. The young learner, that is, does not talk and read explicitly about categories and theories of experience; he talks and reads about characters, events, and settings. For children, though, these characters, events, and settings, are charged with symbolic meaning because they are tokens standing for unconscious classes and postulations of experience, the sort we can infer from regularities in their behavior. The good and bad fairies are categories of experience, and the triumph of the good fairy is a reassuring generalization about overcoming danger.*

Nor do people outgrow this way of "making narrative do for all." We simply add other ways to it. We only have to listen to each other talking, anywhere from the bedroom to the lecture hall, from the street to our living rooms, to witness the fact that people are language-made, and that we all use language in the form of story all the time in order to tell each other about ourselves.

*James Moffett, *Teaching the Universe of Discourse* (Boston: Houghton Mifflin, 1968) p. 49.

Language is demotic because to become human we need it; it was not invented as a way of passing the time, like a great big crossword puzzle — and the more developed and subtle it becomes the greater is its power. By it we are led to awareness, making intelligible what would otherwise be unintelligible. Language is creative, civilizing. Because this is so we recognize the importance of being brought up with as much command of it as possible, and of the variety of uses to which it can be put.

In gaining that command, in reaching that understanding, we also know that children above all need a wide experience of spoken language. Their ability to come to grips with the literary uses of language — their ability at *storying*, at "making narrative do for all" — depends upon this primary experience. Literature is built on the bedrock of language-in-speech. What we expect from literature, what we are able to take from it and bring to it, depends entirely on what we have come to expect of speech. If our knowledge of the spoken word is restricted (and many children's is) to simple question and answer uttered in tones of only a few kinds — crude commands, instructions, admonitions like "Don't do that," "Go and get your breakfast," "You are a stupid kid" — determined by the need to express the least of human pleasures and requirements, then literary language, when it is eventually met, seems as strange as an unknown foreign language to alien ears. The link between speech and literature is of course forged early in life through storytelling and reading aloud, which prepare children for that unique relationship with language and form they will encounter when they read for themselves.

Which brings us to the subject of "form."

What is it that makes the literary use of language so important? Simply this: The basic unit of language is not the word, but the phrase. And the basic unit of sense-making is not the phrase but the combination of phrases into a form that contains information that tells us what happened, to whom it happened, and why it happened.

What happens, to whom, and why is a classic definition of Story. And Story is everywhere. No culture, no civilization, no tribe nor human group has ever been found that does not use Story as its basic and usual means of communication. Once we have language, it seems, we use it to tell stories.

Story can, of course, take various subforms. These range from one-sentence stories we call jokes and wise sayings, through gossip — the story of our lives told in daily episodes by our tongues — to the most profound and complicated structures we call novels and poems and plays. (Chapter twelve looks more closely at this aspect of storying.) And there are differences between stories we tell (with all the help of facial expression, voice tones, and the ability to maneuver what we say and how we say it to suit our audience at the very moment of telling) and story as written, when the reader has to supply so much of the dramatic color, and must match himself to the author, rather than the author adjusting the tale and its telling to fit the listener.

This is a point we must come back to, for it is vital in the making of literary readers. For now, let us concentrate on the primacy of language used in the form of Story: the means by which we talk to ourselves about ourselves, and the only means of communication that can make sense *to the whole population all at once*, no matter what an individual's personal gifts or limits. Give a person a language, and through story we can talk about anything and everything to do with life, not to mention what we think we know and believe about death. Give a person a language, and he can communicate with others through story.

Inevitably, of course, some people succeed at this better than others. Most can succeed at it in speech and not in writing. The writer's gift is to orchestrate words in print better than the rest of us. Reading therefore extends our own capacity with language. Instead of struggling alone, locked in our inadequacy with words, we couple with the writer in an act of verbal creation in which communication is consummated. And so, as C. S. Lewis noted in his useful little book, *An Experiment in Criticism*, in reading literature we become a thousand different people and yet remain ourselves. We do not merge with the writer; we simply benefit by the addition of his gift. Once aware of that possibility we do not lightly reject what literature has to offer. For unless we possess within our own being all the power of imagination we want and need, unless we are satisfied that our individual gift with language can find all the meaning and significance we look for, unless we have all the time, energy and ability to experience all we wish to experience, unless we believe we can do all this unaided, then we had better pay heed to literature.

Given a chance, children soon discover this and pay heed. They are happy enough to listen to stories, and go to books, once they have met them, with no apparent difficulty. The trouble is that their willingness is fragile. It not only needs encouragement, but it can easily be weakened and distracted. What we are witnessing when we meet a child who rejects books, or is indifferent to them, is not a child who was born like that, but rather someone who has become like that because of the way books have been presented to him, usually by adults — which brings us at once face to face with the importance of understanding how we can introduce books to children in such a way that they remain attractive, something to be valued and enjoyed.

Quite as strong, and a more subtle reason, why some children reject literature, especially when this happens in adolescence, is that they have not been taught well enough the different ways language can be used, and, therefore, the different ways of reading. In science, for example, the effort is to find a fixed, unchanging meaning for words. And so in scientific language — in all purely fact-communicating uses of language — we try to employ words in as objective and unvarying a way as possible. When we read it, we want to receive the information quickly and clearly. All the attention is on the information itself. Anything else is simply a distraction. When words fail to behave themselves, as they frequently do, scientists tend to invent a new language composed of tightly defined symbols in order to express their thoughts and discoveries.

Language in literature, however, tries to fuse disparate experiences into coherent wholes. It is the whole poem, the whole story, the whole play or novel that matters. Within the whole, the subjective and objective, the personal and specific with the general and universal, are brought together. Literary language is vital, shifting, fluid; it looks constantly for new structures, new combinations that create new meanings. It employs images, especially metaphor, in order to say several things at once. It thrives on ambiguity, irony, paradox, which bring the disparate and hitherto unconnected into relationship, revealing new shades of meaning, or refreshing the worn, the tired, the clichéd.

Thus literary language is living language, rebellious against imprisonment in the past but ever ready to feed on what has gone before. In *Little Gidding* T. S. Eliot gives us some lines that express what I mean not just by saying it but by demonstrating it too:

Last season's fruit is eaten
And the fullfed beast shall kick the empty pail.
For last year's words belong to last year's language
And next year's words await another voice.

This is why we quite often find that literary uses of language deliberately explode dictionary definitions, and by the particular way a particular author uses words, selects and orders them, they take on a highly personal color we call *style*.

In exercising his art the literary writer is an amanuensis of his time. Through his work we are brought into direct contact not only with ourselves and our contemporaries but, through the literature of the past, with the whole long line of humankind. Not all writers by any means reach down into the depths of experience and record it for us as profoundly as those we call great. Some even mislead and confuse us. But at its best this is what literature does.

Everyone who is a reader has his own list of books which at different times opened his eyes anew. High on mine is D. H. Lawrence's *Sons and Lovers*. It was like an elutriate, that book, when I first read it at the age of fifteen, clarifying myself for myself as well as showing me I was not alone. I suddenly realized that there were others who thought and felt as I did. I was never quite the same again. A bit later in life *Pride and Prejudice* moved me quite as deeply but in a different way. Here was a world and a collection of people so strange that I was spellbound with fascination, as an explorer might stand staring at a new land and an alien people. But the further I went into that foreign domain the more I began to recognize facets of behavior, motivations, characters, which struck familiar chords. Jane Austen taught me the power of literature to open up different worlds, strange people, while at the same time making it possible for

me to find the relationship of those worlds, those people, to the
world and people I know and belong to.

Two other voices summarize these aspects of the value of
literature: that it is conciliatory, comforting us in our shared
humanity; and that it is subversive, challenging our prejudices
and ingrained attitudes, our complacency. First, here is C. S.
Lewis in *An Experiment in Criticism:*

> This, so far as I can see, is the specific value or good of literature
> . . . it admits us to experiences other than our own. They are not,
> any more than our personal experiences, all equally worth having.
> Some, as we say, "interest" us more than others. The causes of
> this interest are naturally extremely various and differ from one
> man to another; it may be the typical (and we say "How true!")
> or the abnormal (and we say "How strange!"); it may be the
> beautiful, the terrible, the awe-inspiring, the exhilarating, the
> pathetic, the comic, or the merely piquant. Literature gives the
> *entrée* to them all.*

And now Lionel Trilling in his Introduction to an edition
of *Huckleberry Finn,* another of those books that stands high on
my own list of life-enhancing and life-changing works of literature. Twain's masterpiece was once barred, as ridiculously it is
again,

> . . . . from certain libraries and schools for its alleged sub-
> version of morality. The authorities had in mind the book's
> endemic lying, the petty thefts, the denigrations of respecta-
> bility and religion, the bad language and the bad grammar. We
> smile at the excessive care, yet in point of fact *Huckleberry Finn*
> is indeed a subversive book — no one who reads thoughtfully
> the dialectic of Huck's great moral crisis will ever again be
> wholly able to accept without some question and some irony
> the assumptions of the respectable morality by which he lives,
> nor will ever again be certain that what he considers the clear
> dictates of moral reason are not merely the engrained customary
> beliefs of his time and place.†

*C. S. Lewis, *An Experiment in Criticism* (Cambridge: Cambridge University
Press, 1961) pp. 139-140.
†Lionel Trilling, Introduction to *The Adventures of Huckleberry Finn* (New
York: Rinehart, 1948) p. xiii.

Somehow we have to bring children to an understanding of all this potential that lies in literature. But it is an understanding that comes to most people only gradually, and only when there is first of all a groundwork of stories told and read aloud to build on.

LITERATURE AS ACTION

Children come to reading for amusement. If a book does not yield immediate pleasure they tend to lay it aside. But that is a superficial requirement. Whether consciously or not, like adults they take much more than trite satisfaction from what they read. Before one becomes a mature, avid reader, however — one of those, as Trilling puts it, who can read *thoughtfully* — one has to become conscious of literature as an active agent, part of the chemistry of daily life. And there is an unfortunate implication in the way some people talk about reading which suggests that it is a substitute for action, a pastime that decorates the idle margins of the serious business of living. They seem to regard literature as a secondary experience (if they think of it as an experience at all), more akin to being a peeping Tom, an impotent voyeur, rather than being one of the healthy, active people who get on with real living.

That this is an attitude often taken up in unthinking ignorance of the physiological and psychological facts does not help. Children who have been instilled with it will ask why they should be bothered to read literature.

The answers are worth rehearsing, even though we have touched on some of them in passing already.

First of all, no one can engage "directly" in the whole range of human experiences, not even the full range of those thought worth having. There is neither time nor opportunity in one life. But even supposing there were, it would still not be possible. How can a Western-born white man, to take an extreme example, experience directly what it means to be a black Central African? Or vice versa? He can try by going to live in a black Central African home and getting as close to his host's way of life as can be contrived. But he will soon discover that even then all the accidents of birth, upbringing, education, and social history will prevent his truly knowing the very thing he wants to know — how it all actually feels to his host. To get really close he must make an act of imaginative projection, and have communicated to him the inner realities which only the African can know. He can achieve this by experiencing it through the stories, the poems, the vocal and written literature created by his African host and people. In this respect engagement in literature is an action more effective than any other open to us.

Nor can we directly experience what it was like to be alive in an historical time — in, say, Elizabethan England — because the space-time barrier prevents it. The best way of gaining some sense of what life used to be like is through the literature of the time. It is true that painting, music, architecture, and surviving artifacts all help, but not as literature can, for literature is about the re-creation of the texture of experience in the way that Richard Hoggart explains in Chapter one.

Most children can easily see that they need Story if they want to know what it is like to be a sportsman, a nurse, a burglar, a pilot, a patient in a hospital. There are a thousand and one possibilities in life which children quite as much as adults would like to experience and know about, but which they cannot by any means that are emotionally as well as intellectually informative and affective, other than by the dramatic enactments which literature offers. Once this is discovered and acknowledged reading takes on an attraction and an importance that extends beyond pastime pleasure, a substitute for "doing."

But there are more telling, if more complex, considerations yet. Everyone is aware of the number of courses of action open to us at any one time, even allowing for hidden impulses, unconscious drives and all the rest of the unwitting controls which form our actions. Without an ability to select when faced with these choices we would be like demented dogs chasing every attractive smell that reaches our noses in complete confusion of purpose. Our ability to make choices depends largely on the power, quality and range of our imagination. In other words, to make sense of life-situations and to make intelligent decisions when we meet them, we need to have pondered the various possibilities either before the situations arise or with speed and sureness when they arise. For this reason we are constantly setting up in our minds various imagined and possible events so that we can explore various possible ways of handling them and the consequences. These explorations may be based on the typical, on the specific (things we have witnessed, rerun and edited in our imaginations like old movies), and on actual, known circumstances we are about to encounter. Children's play is organized like this too. Primitive war dances, fertility rites, hunting games, and all those rituals human beings develop in their corporate as well as their private lives are all "trials" of this storying kind. Conversations which are controlled by such phrases as "Supposing it's this way ... then ..." are doing the same job for us. And literature is part of that essential human behavior. It engages us in pre-enactments and re-enactments. The situations are invented (or adapted from observation) by the author and we the readers both observe and get imaginatively involved in the playing out of the life-in-the-story. We even react as though it were all happening to us by feeling sad or happy, frightened or angry, amused or scandalized, and so on.

Literature is therefore strongly influential in organizing and sifting the attitudes which inform and guide our choices of overt action. I do not mean to say that having read about a character we then go out and behave in a precisely similar fashion. Rather, I mean that literature helps us clarify, helps us to awareness. And *becoming aware* (a never-finishing process of intelligent life) is in itself action.

But this is to discuss imaginative action only in relation to circumstances in which we must or wish to get involved. There are many actions we deliberately avoid, and yet they interest us because they are part of human experience. Look, for example, at the fascination murder holds for many people. Few, if any of us, want to be involved in murder, but the brutal act of one person killing another, the motives for doing so, the personal and social consequences, all hold our attention, as newspaper editors well know and exploit. Literature provides a way of participating. We are Raskolnikov in *Crime and Punishment*, and his hunter too. Simenon may be read by many people for amusement only, but if we read him thoughtfully he shows us a variety of insights into the kind of crises that push people into criminal acts. We may have no belief in God, but through the poetry of Gerard Manley Hopkins we get into the skin of a man who has and see with his eyes, think his thoughts, know his belief in both its certainty and its doubt.

Nor is it only great literature that does this for us. Even writing that we reject for its shallowness, its lack of penetration, demands in the very act of rejection that we match what we know of life, and of other literature, against what this writer offers — though, to hammer the point again, this is only true when we are reading thoughtfully.

All these different ways in which literature functions have enormous value for children, as for adults. Children are forming attitudes, finding points of reference, building concepts, forming images to think with, all of which interact to form a basis for decision-making judgment, for understanding, for sympathy with the human condition. Literary experience feeds the imagination, that faculty by which we come to grips with the astonishing amount of data which assails our everyday lives, and find patterns of meaning in it.

"Don't confuse motion with action," Hemingway is said to have advised Ms. Dietrich, and he was right. There has been little obvious motion but plenty of action when a child finds through reading a book that a dull day is transformed because he has met a talking pig (whom everybody knows to be a fiction) and a spider that can write (which nobody believes ever happens) discussing the nature of life in Charlotte's Web. And there is more to be gained from an imaginary nineteenth-century boy floating down the Mississippi on a raft with a fleeing black slave than a good deal of everyday, "direct" experience can give, no matter how much of what so often passes for purposeful action is packed into the same time as it takes to read Huckleberry Finn.

No one but an obsessed fanatic would suggest that reading is all or enough in itself. But a reader who gets as far as enjoying Huck or Charlotte does not question the value of literature or the time spent on reading it. And getting children this far is the first aim of all the work we do with children and books. They won't, any of them, get there on their own. They need help and encouragement, opportunity and guidance. They need to be led to books which will expand their sense of what it means to read fully and closely, and be led by methods which do not suffocate the desire to go on reading so thoughtfully. After parents, who all too often have not got this far themselves, teachers and librarians carry the responsibility for bringing children and books together. Though they cannot succeed on their own, they are the ones who need to be most aware of what they are doing and how they are doing it when they try to help children grow into literary readers.

III

The Making of a Literary Reader

Readers are made, not born. No one comes into the world already disposed for or against words in print. It is not easy, however, to separate out all the complicated circumstances, stages of psychological development, individual idiosyncrasies, and adult and peer influences that interweave and form a child's literary development. But I want in this chapter to try to unravel some of the features that are usually considered most relevant. For clarity's sake I have grouped them under headings, but I cannot stress enough how artificial these categories are. The influences described never work in isolation but interact in varying combinations and strengths depending on an individual's personal history. People are not machines and are never completely alike; discussions of the kind that follow are only useful when we remember this.

SOCIALIZATION

One of those jargon words invented and enjoyed by sociologists and educational theorists, "socialization" happens to be more convenient than most and a little less objectionable. The Penguin *Dictionary of Psychology* defines it as "the process by which the individual is adapted to his social environment, and becomes a recognized, cooperating, and efficient member of it." That is to say, socialization is the name we give to the way children learn to behave like the adults around them, taking for their own the attitudes, values, customs, and mores of the social group to which they belong.

What we know about this process has implications for our theme. Quite obviously, as most children spend their infant years aware of very few people, usually members of their family, it is from them — parents, brothers and sisters, attendant relatives and friends — that they learn the primary adaptive lessons. Naturally, how these people regard books, how much they read and talk about what they have read, how many books they buy and borrow, keep about them and value, will be part of the way of life taken on by their children.

But this is by no means all there is to it. The quality of the talk that goes on in a family, especially perhaps at relaxed times during meals, in leisure activities, and before bed, strikes deep, to the roots of a child's proper growth. When the talk is rich in content, when it is spoken in a variety of tones and is verbally colorful and inventive, a child is being prepared for the possibilities of language. Whereas when the talk is limited, anemic, verbally and tonally narrow, just the opposite is true; a deprivation occurs that will later show itself in difficulties in learning to read, in writing, in coping with social situations where speech is essential.

Within this oral tradition the socializing part played by storytelling and reading aloud is central to the encouragement of literacy. Listening to stories, poems, nursery rhymes, nonsense, while occupied with a loved adult in a comforting activity, acclimatizes the infant imagination to the idea of character, the structuring of events in story, the shape and rhythms of prose and poetry. By it too is nourished stamina — the focus of attention and concentration over a period of time that reading calls for. There is no surprise in the increasingly weighty evidence presented in ever more numerous research papers which confirms that children from homes where books are plentiful, speech rich, and reading aloud a regular and frequent experience, tend to look forward to learning to read and indeed often arrive at school already able to do so. While children from homes where speech has a narrow range and books are absent tend to be the ones who have difficulty.

A book-conscious home lays a solid foundation, but there are socializing factors which may undermine it and which, of course, further disable those children who lack such basic support. These have been frequently noted and I need only mention them briefly here.

1. Children born into large families or who are brought up in institutions are at a disadvantage. They have less opportunity than children in small families for sustained conversation *with adults*, and it is speech exchange with mature people that matters most rather than exchanges with other children. Similarly, they have less opportunity to be read to on their own, which has a different quality from being read to as one of a group. Thus we can find that seven-year-olds from a large family may be on average as much as one year or more behind those from small families in reading attainment.

2. Living in overcrowded conditions adversely affects reading progress. There is a lack of quiet, and of private places where children can escape from noise, movement, visitors, TV, to find an atmosphere that helps reading. Large families often have to live in overcrowded conditions, thus worsening the problems described in (1) above, which are further worsened if the family is financially poor and linguistically limited.

3. No family lives in isolation unless it is remarkably cut off geographically. Spreading out from the doorstep is a wider social group whose influence comes to bear on children, particularly after they are old enough to wander at large on their own.

4. Television adds its potent influence to those of family and friends. Indeed, for many children the language and stories heard and seen on TV far outweigh in quantity and influence the speech-and-story of the people the children live among. This is why it is vital to keep track of TV output, especially of programs like *Sesame Street* in the United States and *Jackanory* in Britain, which try to act responsibly towards children, their language, and literature.

All these influences are at work before a child goes to school, yet until quite recently we have behaved as though good teaching in good schools (whatever we conceived that "good" to consist in) was, if not enough, then the best that could be done to compensate for the disabilities of verbally impoverished children.

Now we have begun to admit, though we still do not do enough about it, that the early years before a child goes to school have a permanent, lifelong effect, and that if we want to improve "educational standards," and certainly if we want to make literary readers, we must get at the social roots of deprivation. While government funds were available in the United States, Head Start and Home Start programs were steps in those directions. In short, education must go home, must involve parents and the conditions in which families live far more intimately than has ever been achieved before except by the wealthy, already articulate and literate few.

There is, however, no reason to despair of schools having an influence on children from subliterate and illiterate homes, even as things still are, otherwise the short history of universal education would be much sorrier than it is. Schools themselves, and libraries, are socializing agents, and though the children will already have formed basic attitudes important to literacy before they arrive in front of teachers or librarians, they are, except in some extreme and rare cases, far from beyond hope. Provided, that is, we keep in mind that whatever goes on in school and library is compared by children with what goes on in their own homes, and that when those influences clash, whether by default rather than by design, the children are sometimes damaged by the conflict.

A child's life cannot, without unhappy consequences, be separated into two unconnected compartments in which, on the one side, teachers take no account of home and neighborhood, and parents, on the other side, know little and care less about the institutions where their children spend a considerable part of their days. Taking as the classic model of this dilemma the "uprooted and anxious" boy from a poor home, Richard Hoggart years ago described the far-reaching tensions of such a dual existence and includes this passage about the literary side effects:

> Such a boy is between two worlds of school and home; and they meet at few points. Once at the grammar-school, he quickly learns to make use of a pair of different accents, perhaps even two different apparent characters and differing standards of value. Think of his reading material, for example: at home he

> sees strewn around, and reads regularly himself, magazines which are never mentioned at school, which seem not to belong to the world to which school introduces him; at school he hears about and reads books never mentioned at home. When he brings those books into the house they do not take their place with other books which the family are reading, for often there are none or almost none; his books look, rather, like strange tools.*

The implications are burdensome, raising questions which, as Hoggart goes on to point out,

> have to do with the importance of roots, of unconscious roots, to all of us as individuals; they have to do with those major social developments of our times towards centralization and a kind of classlessness; and they have to do with the relationship between cultural and intellectual matters and the beliefs by which men try to shape their lives.†

They are questions which reach beyond the confines of this present book, but they do point to some conclusions we need to take into account.

First, teachers and librarians cannot afford to turn a blind eye to the literature a child is brought up with at home, no matter how anemic and worthless it may seem to be. It is what the child knows, and "work from the known to the unknown" is an old rule of teaching as true today as it ever was. When children come from book-conscious homes, this presents no difficulty; school is then hardly more than an extension and intensification of home reading activities. For children from non-book homes the transition is not so smooth. By discovering what they read — probably comics, cheap paperbacks like the series about Nancy Drew and the Hardy Boys, newspapers, and special-interest magazines — and by talking about it *from knowledge* (which means we must pay the child the compliment we expect him to pay us and read what he tells us about) teacher/librarian and pupil find common ground, a point of departure for the child, into the unfamiliar. So a relationship of trust can be forged

---

*Richard Hoggart, *The Uses of Literacy* (London: Chatto and Windus, 1957) p. 296.
†Ibid.

out of mutual respect and interest which makes a child far more willing to be led where the teacher/librarian would take him. And, just as important, the sharp division between home and school is blurred a little and the tensions Hoggart talked about are eased.

Secondly, schools need to make deliberate, carefully planned efforts to awaken parents to the part they play in the literary education of their children by drawing them whenever possible into the work done in school, and by teachers going out into the community to work there alongside parents. In areas of chronic illiteracy this may need to be conducted with as much energy as is given to in-school work. We have hardly begun to touch this aspect of educational strategy in most places, and indeed it is a daunting prospect for those teachers who face all the problems endemic in the neighborhoods where literary impoverishment is most acute, the heavily populated, least prosperous inner-city areas.

Nevertheless, there are ways to begin, however modestly. Through pre-school playgroups and parent-teacher organizations, for example; by using school bookshops, preferably run by a team of parents, teachers, and children working together; by teachers' visits to their pupils' homes. In such ways parents and teachers can get together and learn from each other, breaking down the barriers of mistrust that often exist between the "expert" professionals and the "ignorant" nonprofessionals. It would be starry-eyed to imagine that we will ever reach into every home, or every home will ever reach into every institutionalized school. There will always be a depressingly high percentage of intransigent parents and arrogant professionals — and those perhaps the very ones most in need of help. But it is worth remembering that most parents and most teachers care deeply about their children's education, and will go to considerable lengths to promote it if they are given a reasonable chance.

Thirdly, because it is the socializing that goes on in pre-school years that matters above all we must, as a society and as professionals with special responsibilities within that society, do more to put matters right at this stage. This is why the work of public children's librarians who concentrate their efforts on preschool children and their parents is of such enormous importance.

At the other end of the childhood ages, teachers of adolescents can — though not enough by any means do — play a role in preparing future parents for their responsibilities. It is now commonplace for fifteen- and sixteen-year-olds to be given courses dealing with the making and raising of a family. Far from commonplace in those courses, when it ought to be a central topic, is a study of the language and literary development of infants. Schools which do include such a study find a strong and enthusiastic response from many pupils, especially when the work involves these pupils, as it always should, in storytelling and reading aloud to young children. Discussion of picturebooks and stories for the early years is often conducted with far more genuine feeling and intelligent argument than is discussion of the literature set for study by these same teenagers, and the rediscovery (or sometimes the first discovery) of the pleasures of nursery rhyme, of folk and fairy tales, of nonsense verse and story leads in itself to a realization of their importance and function in our lives.

Quite obviously, however, everything rests in the end on the extent to which people grow up to be avid, thoughtful readers. Which brings us back to the role teachers play in that process. And once again fundamental features mark out the landscape.

1. Just as non-reading children are made by non-reading parents, so the issue is compounded by non-reading teachers. Unless a school has on its staff at least some adults who enjoy books and enjoy talking to children about what they read, it is hardly likely that it will be successful in helping children become readers. Lip service (and reading gets plenty of that in educational circles) is not enough.

2. Surroundings matter. Whether or not reading is an activity given space and the kind of physical conditions it requires — just as sport is given the provision it needs, and other specialist activities — how books are presented and displayed as objects, how easily accessible they are: considerations like these, dealt

with in detail in later chapters, affect the attitude of children towards books and reading.

3. In the nature of school life there are biases which, if not guarded against, turn children off.

Ironically, the most dangerous bias exists because of the usefulness and convenience of books themselves. The printed word in book form even yet, despite all the advances in electronic means of communication, has no rival as the most efficient, inexpensive and effective way to teach and to learn. Textbooks — which are no more than teaching machines — supplementary "readers," instruction manuals, reference works, tomes teeming with problems for the pupils to solve — all these plus a plethora of information books on any and every topic imaginable: in teaching session after teaching session, day after day, school tasks are administered through books. We ought not to be surprised by two logical consequences.

First, all but the most avid child readers will want to escape from books and reading in their leisure time.

Secondly, because books are so often used as a means of instruction, of fact-finding and didacticism, children too often come to suppose that this is the sole nature and purpose of all books, that this is how all books must be read, except, of course, for those outlaw delights like comics and the series pleasures which you can very easily tell because they quite deliberately bear no relation whatever in their appearance to the kind of book from which children are made to learn in school.

In short, we can fall into the trap of teaching children only one way of reading: that which dutifully seeks the acquisition of information to be used for other ends: Reading as a tool that enables us to do something else, rather than reading which has invaluable ends and purposes in itself.

4. Out of this fact-grubbing, didactic bias grows another. The abuse and misuse of literature. Some examples to indicate what I mean:

I once worked with an English teacher who taught twelve-year-olds to parse by setting for sample text the opening paragraph of J. M. Falkner's novel *Moonfleet*. This extraordinary assault on a fine old children's book has ever since stood for me as the epitome of the scholastic abuse of literature.

But it was no less misguided, only more crude, than the commonplace practice of setting passages thieved from literature for comprehension exercises. (What color was the pirate's coat? How do you know? Why did Jim kill Israel Hands?) Or for other drills. (Write a brief character sketch of Long John Silver. List all the unfamiliar words you can find in *Treasure Island*. Write a letter, as if you were Jim Hawkins, telling your mother you have just found the treasure.) Every English textbook I can think of abuses literature in this treacherous fashion.

And this is only the beginning. Close on such parade-ground excitements comes the popular sport of plundering for projects. The children are "doing," let us say, a group project on dogs. They are encouraged to hunt out anything and everything that so much as mentions them and the bits thus mined are assiduously transcribed into project folders. We'll be sure not to miss Philippa Pearce's *A Dog So Small*: there are a few sentences about borzois on page 13 and there are all those bits about puppies in Chapter 14. They'll go well with some extracts from *Dogs: Records, Stars, Feats and Facts* [Roger Caras and Pamela C. Graham, published in 1979 by Harcourt Brace]. Naturally, we shall want the fight scene from *White Fang*, something from Eric Knight's *Lassie Come Home*, and just for fun we'll include a squib about Mouse Fawley's garbage dog from *The Eighteenth Emergency* by Betsy Byars to put alongside a passage about mongrels from the *World Book Encyclopedia*. All is raked together into a kind of anthological ragbag which passes for "research," for a "child-centered learning situation." And everything is set down without reference to context, or author's intention, or the difference between one kind of writing and reading and another — between the naked facts and figures of an encyclopedia and Betsy Byars's recreation of a flesh-and-blood boy. There are teachers who make sensitive use of project work, not just as a way of training children in study as a means of exploring a subject, but also as a way of teaching about the different kinds of writing there are. But I have seen too many examples of the misuse of literature in this way to think that what I am describing is rare or a parody of the real state of affairs in many schools.

We are talking in fact about the difference between "using" and "receiving" literature. C. S. Lewis made the distinction in *An Experiment in Criticism*:

> A work of (whatever) art can be either "received" or "used." When we "receive" it we exert our senses and imagination and various other powers according to a pattern invented by the artist. When we "use" it we treat it as assistance for our own activities.*

I think what we must understand is that literature is not simply a resource, in the educationally trendy and jargonistic use of that word, but is *of itself*, an experience to be entered into, to be shared and contemplated. And this is what we must teach children, *by discovery*, it is.

5. Sometimes even the teaching of literature in a school becomes itself an adverse bias. This comes about through the puritanical narrowness of the "official" literature approved for study. In an understandable desire to give children only the best, we have too often undermined the very thing we are trying to achieve by interpreting the "best" as meaning only one kind of writing, rather than the best of all kinds.

In the past twenty or thirty years a growing number of teachers all through the educational system, from kindergarten to university, have challenged this situation. They have examined their own reading habits honestly and drawn unsettling conclusions about what should be expected of children as readers. They have thought through their own development from childhood and acted on the implications this revealed for their work as teachers. They have understood, to begin with, that the traditional "classics" are not the only texts worth close reading, but that there is a rich body of so-called "children's books" which merits just as much consideration by adults as well as by

*C. S. Lewis, *An Experiment in Criticism* (Cambridge: Cambridge University Press, 1961) p. 88.

children. They have noted the separation between what they as
teachers tend to bring into the classroom and the popular reading
they and their pupils and students do outside the classroom and
have looked for ways of making the best literary use of both.
They have compared their school and library stocks with the
backgrounds from which their children come and seen the need
for a recognition of literature which gives these cultural backgrounds a voice. Most of all they have reconsidered what happens
when we respond to what we have read, and how these responses
can be given outlets and be channeled into educationally
valuable discussion.

They have realized, these teachers and librarians, that what
matters is not that children should read only those books adults
have decided will be "good for them," but that adults and
children together should share all that they read, and discover
together what it is they find that is entertaining and revealing,
recreative, re-enactive, and engaging.

Before we leave the socializing process we must note one
more factor that will be further explored in a later chapter.
From the time children go to school they mix with large numbers
of their contemporaries, and these peers exert an ever-increasing
influence as the school years pass. Some children are swayed
more than others by the attitudes, opinions, behavior of friends
and fellows, but none escapes unaffected, not even the outsider,
the loner. And this is something teachers and librarians cannot
ignore, for it plays an inevitable part in children's corporate and
individual responses to them and to what they are trying to
achieve.

Thus teachers especially, because they have a captive audience, find themselves along with parents and a child's peers, one
of a triumvirate of main socializing agents in a child's life. They
are so placed that they can influence the other two, while the
responsibility society puts upon them provides opportunities as
well as resources which give them advantages over both parents
and peers in helping children become literary readers.

STAGES OF GROWTH

So far I have outlined some of the social conditions which affect a child's reading development. I want to turn now to another aspect: that which has to do with psychological growth.

Just as we can recognize stages of physical growth so we can isolate, rather crudely but nevertheless usefully, stages of psychological growth that have relevance to our theme. They are at work at the same time as social influences. They may harmonize or they may clash, but they do not operate separately. A shift in one — when a child moves from one school to another, for example, or even from one teacher to another — will cause a shift in the other — a new teacher whom a child likes and who likes reading can, for example, change almost overnight a child's attitude to reading stories.

What, then, are these "stages"? What should we expect of children as they pass through them? What do we learn about the development of literary taste? As a starting point here are two authoritative voices. The first, Dr. Levin Schücking in his pioneer study *The Sociology of Literary Taste*, suggests stages of literary growth as he observed them:

> The child's intelligence as it first begins to develop is most easily attracted by the description of familiar day-to-day incidents, usually regarding its own life; when its imagination awakes, without corresponding development of the critical faculty, it gets a taste for fairy stories; with the awakening of youthful urge to activity it finds fascination in tales of adventure; puberty brings interest in the dreamy and sentimental; maturity brings a more realistic make-up; greater experience of life and the growing sense of reality bring a dislike of highly colored representation of things and a preference for keen and satirical observation over the merely fanciful. Most adults feel the awakening of interest in biography and a diminution at the same time of the fondness for fiction.*

This brief sketch was enlarged by Dr. Jacqueline Burgoyne, who adds details noted by other investigators and confirmed by her own studies when, with Professor Peter Mann, she researched in Britain the reasons why people read, what they read, the social backgrounds of those who read, and why they borrowed or

*Levin Schücking, *The Sociology of Literary Taste*, 2nd ed. (London: Routledge and Kegan Paul, 1966) p. 78.

bought books. Her conclusions appeared in *Books and Reading*:

> Schücking suggests stages in reading development to which we
> have added another intermediate stage because Schücking was
> concerned only with literary development. He suggests that a
> young child is first attracted to reading by finding that the real
> world which he has so far perceived and experienced can also
> be found in stories and books. At this stage children like stories
> to be about themselves and the things which they have experi-
> enced, and a child's very first books may consist only of illus-
> trations and text describing familiar incidents, as the first
> "Ladybird" books do. At this stage pictures are important; they
> link visual and verbal symbols and their importance declines as
> the child grasps more of the symbolic significance of words and
> is able to build up his own imaginative pictures from verbal
> stimulus. Words describe more explicitly yet leave the imagina-
> tion free to work and in adult books illustrations, unless they
> have an aesthetic appeal, are included only where a diagram
> would be shorthand for a longer verbal explanation.
>
> A second stage, Schücking suggests, is reached at the time at
> which the young child's powers of imagination are very active.
> He has begun to perceive experience beyond the home and
> local environment and to conceive of processes and emotions
> more exciting than everyday life; this is the world of fancies,
> Santa Claus, "human" animals like Winnie-the-Pooh and Peter
> Rabbit, and Daleks and is often shown by the way in which a
> young child is able to carry on a sustained relationship with an
> imaginary friend or animal. At this stage schools recognize that
> much is learned through play; new roles are tried out and a
> child begins to enter imaginatively into other worlds. Stories
> and books are an important part of this process.
>
> The development of imaginative powers and perception is not
> uniform; we all know adults whom we consider unimaginative
> or perhaps over-imaginative and little is known about the way
> in which these differences occur. Studies of deprived children
> suggest that those who do not receive the necessary stimulus in
> early childhood may never be able to compensate. In one sense
> learning is a chain process; we hang a new piece of knowledge,
> technique of doing or thinking on something learned previously.
> If the first links are missing it is difficult for schools to make
> good the deficiencies.
>
> Schücking stresses that at this stage "imagination flows with-

out critical faculty." This is when children are not really concerned with scientific truth; they believe in Father Christmas anyway, even if there lurks the suspicion that there is something rather fishy about it all. Perhaps an openly expressed disbelief in his activities is one of the marks of the passing of this stage.

At the next step facts become increasingly important. Teaching methods which stress "finding out" and personal discovery are based upon a thesis of Piaget's, a Swiss psychologist, that at this stage of "concrete operations" children think in factual terms which are an essential preliminary to abstract and deductive thought. Although some children will have already become inveterate readers, in their spare time up until puberty activity is generally more important than reflective thinking. It is possible that this is why historical writers such as Rosemary Sutcliff and Alfred Duggan are so popular at this stage; fantasy is linked with factual material and much modern fiction for this age is increasingly realistic, for example, the writing of J. Rowe Townsend and William Mayne. This period of latency, where, if Freud's framework is valid, emotion plays a relatively small part, is disregarded by Schücking because this may be the time when children are least interested in works of a literary nature.

Puberty, he describes as "dreamy and sentimental" and though this may seem a far cry from the teenagers of the 1960's [or the 1980's] we would recognize that adolescence brings an awakening of emotions, idealism and commitment to a romantic ideal. For those who are active readers there is plenty to read and teachers have commented to us upon the amount and diversity of reading done by "readers," more often girls than boys. In one term this may vary from Jane Austen to Alan Sillitoe, Hardy and Scott to Margaret Drabble, with a regular dose of [teenage magazines like] Valentine thrown in.

By adolescence the die is usually cast and those who never read rarely come to find pleasure in reading in itself, although they may be helped toward a more mature use of books for the extension of other activities. . . .

Perhaps we should make a distinction at this stage between fiction which comforts, reinforcing the reader's ideas and values, or provides him with an escape from the dull real world where people rarely "live happily ever after" and fiction which challenges readers to think and to face reality. Teenage escape reading is often found through magazines.

Transition to maturity is characterized by Schücking as a "dislike for highly colored representations" as a result of greater experience of life and a growing sense of reality. This results, he says, "in an awakening of interest in biography and a diminution at the same time of fondness for fiction." This is certainly true of a large number of readers, although the transition is rarely absolute. We continue to enjoy a certain number of books whose only purpose is distraction, but they are not our complete diet.*

These two passages serve as introduction, but there are modifications to be added at a number of points.

1.   It is a mistake to suppose that these broad stages of development precisely correspond to clear-cut chronological or "reading" ages — that they do not raises difficulties for teachers faced with large groups of children who, though they may be the same age within a year, will certainly differ greatly in their stages of reading development. The principle we can adopt to ease the problem is that we should provide in school at least as much opportunity, if not more, for individual reading, and individual response between teacher and child, as for corporate reading activities. And these activities must take place against a background of book stocks that are very wide in range of difficulty, subject-content, and storytelling treatment. Much wider than either we think necessary or than most classroom-based book stocks usually are. And we should make great use of pairing between children — who will often select each other — so that an able and fluent reader can read with one who is less developed.

2.   The stages are not cut off from one another, are not sharply defined. Indeed they often rub along together. A child may enjoy *Frog and Toad Are Friends* by Arnold Lobel because it is easy, a favorite now well within his skill, and *Flat Stanley* by Jeff Brown because it is "new" to him and just right for the stage of reading difficulty he has reached, while also showing a strong interest in factual information, about, say, dinosaurs, which according to Schücking's model would predominate only at a later age and stage of development.

*Peter H. Mann and Jacqueline L. Burgoyne, *Books and Reading*, (London: André Deutsch, 1969) pp. 43-47.

Equally, children (like everyone else in fact) may "relapse" for a while, returning to a stage they appear to have left behind. And in pubescence especially they often change direction, quite wildly to adult eyes, reaching at one moment way ahead of themselves towards mature adult books and diving back at another moment into favorite books that belong to a period of their lives they have "grown out of."

These shifts of "mood" have various causes. A change of friends, for example, may realign a child's reading interests so that they suit this new relationship. An emotional crisis at home may send a child burrowing back into the security of well-loved books remembered from happier days. A new and attractive teacher, as I've already said, can accelerate progress. Clearly, therefore, the more teachers know about the children in their charge the better equipped they are to judge not only the reasons for fluctuations but how to respond helpfully to them.

3. Far more difficult to deal with than these fluctuations in growth is arrested development, when a person gets "stuck" at one stage. Many women, for example, never grow as readers beyond the pubescent liking for "dreamy and sentimental" narrative, as the popularity of that kind of story in magazines and books suggests. Men will often stick at the actionful adventure story stage they often get a taste for at about the age of ten. They grow up as readers of James Bond, of dashing thrillers and the blood-and-guts of crude war stories. "Such people," Schücking says, "are in certain respects incapable of progessing beyond the impressions belonging to a period in their lives when their minds were open and receptive to things of this kind. In later years, however, their enjoyment of art is all too often nothing but their own youth which their memory enables them to enjoy all over again."*

There is of course plenty of evidence to suggest that the period when factual information makes its strongest appeal and when literary reading is at its lowest ebb is the stage at which most people are arrested. I wonder if this is not altogether un-

---

*Levin Schücking, *The Sociology of Literary Taste*, 2nd ed. (London: Routledge and Kegan Paul, 1966) p. 79.

related to the fact that this stage immediately precedes puberty, during the last flush of childhood, after which, as teachers of teenagers know too well, young people commonly go through a period of disenchantment with adults and anything they regard as the establishment, a disenchantment that for want of a better target they direct at teachers and schools. Adolescents cannot be led so easily, so unselfconsciously as children, and disenchantment can be a door that closes tight against attempts to reinvigorate dulled literary receptivity. At such times two things are important. That the adolescent has had the good fortune to be brought up during his childhood years in a school and home where literary activity was all we have been and will be suggesting it should be (about which the teacher of adolescents can do nothing); and that he goes on hearing read aloud plenty of literature of various kinds that entertain and connect. Reading aloud, in these circumstances, might be the only contact the adolescent gets with literature, tiding him over to the time when he is prepared to read for himself again.

4. Dr. Burgoyne distinguishes between books which comfort and confirm and those that challenge and subvert. But to make the distinction in this simplistic fashion is misleading because it suggests that books are willy-nilly of one of these two kinds only, each possessing intrinsic, absolute qualities which inevitably affect readers in one way or the other — which is not the case. I touched on this in the previous chapter when I quoted Lionel Trilling's remarks about *Huckleberry Finn*. If we look again at this passage (page 24) we will see that Trilling claims this novel "is indeed a subversive book," but, as I point out, he adds the essential qualifying clause, "no one who reads *thoughtfully* the dialectic of Huck's great moral crisis..." The subversive effect depends entirely on how the reader reads. Fully received by a person open to the book's irony, aware of its incisiveness, and willing to set its moral dialectic against himself, the book is indeed challenging. But it is quite possible for someone to read the story as a vastly entertaining collection of picaresque adventures written with consummate skill and full of "colorful" characters, yet for his own prejudices, beliefs, and customary

morality to remain untouched. Both readers would agree on the
literary quality of the work, but its effects on them would be
different. So how we read is as important as what we read.

The knowing is what matters: knowing how to read according to the demands of the particular book. A reader who is never
challenged, unsettled or moved, who has never realized how
books — intentionally or otherwise on the author's part — can
be subversive, is a reader who does not know how to receive
literature, but only how to use it; does not know how to discover
his responses or how to express them to himself and to others
(a matter we will discuss in Part Four).

So we reach the final stage in the making of a literary reader.
Schücking noted that early step when a child's "imagination
awakes, without corresponding development of the critical
faculty," a step most children make before they reach school age.
Awakening the critical faculty — or more accurately teaching
how to channel and express it, for it is there from the beginning
waiting to be exercised — is therefore part of what the "direct"
teaching of literature is all about. It is pointless, as David
Holbrook among many other teachers has observed, making
"bookworms who will later bore only through pulp." It is not
enough to get children reading regularly and often, though this
is where literary reading begins; not enough, either, to get them
reading books of great quality, though this must itself be a goal.
What ultimately matters is that children be brought to a valued
appreciation that reading is more than a passive pursuit — "Here
I am, amuse me!" — but is a creative activity, an end in itself.

Much has been written about methods directed at making
children critically appreciative readers. One thing I want to say
here so as to avoid misunderstanding. By teaching children to be
critical I do not mean teaching them to pull books apart in a
mechanically formulated way, as though they were dismantling a
piece of machinery. Nor do I mean teaching them to make
comparative judgments about this book being "better" than that,
or one writer being greater than another (they do that without
being taught to). Helen Gardner, no mean critic and no mean
teacher herself, has summed up what needs to be said about such

arid practice in *The Business of Criticism*:

> The attempt to train young people in this kind of discrimination
> seems to me to be a folly, if not a crime. The young need, on
> the one hand, to be encouraged to read for themselves, widely,
> voraciously, and indiscriminately; and, on the other, to be
> helped to read with more enjoyment and understanding what
> their teachers have found to be of value. Exuberance and en-
> thusiasm are proper to the young, as Quintillian remarked:
> "The young should be daring and inventive and should rejoice
> in their inventions, even though correctiveness and severity are
> still to be acquired." And he added that to his mind "the boy
> who gives least promise is the one in whom judgment develops
> in advance of the imagination." True personal discrimination or
> taste develops slowly and probably best unconsciously. It cannot
> be forced by exercises in selecting the good and rejecting the bad
> by the application of stock critical formulas: it may indeed be
> stunted. It comes, if it is to come at all, by growth in under-
> standing and enjoyment of the good. "Principium veritatis
> admirari." Knowledge begins in wonder and wonder will find
> and develop its own proper discipline. True judgment or wis-
> dom in a critic can only come in the same way as all wisdom
> does: "For the very true beginning of her is the desire of disci-
> pline and the care of discipline is love."*

The art of teaching literature so that young people become
critically aware, of helping them, as Helen Gardner puts it, "to
read with more enjoyment and understanding what their teachers
have found to be of value," is a specialist concern. But the
rest of what is involved — the greater part — in making literary
readers is not. Helping children "to read for themselves, widely,
voraciously, and indiscriminately" is something every adult can
do. Certainly, every teacher and librarian not only can but ought
to be involved in offering such help. And this is the fundamental
and practical aspect of children and reading that concerns us in
the rest of this book.

*Helen Gardner, *The Business of Criticism* (Oxford: Oxford University Press,
1959) pp. 13-14.

IV

The Reading Circle, The Reading Adult, and Three Reading Moods

For practical purposes we can summarize what we have said so far under three general headings.

THE READING CIRCLE

There is a circle of cause and effect in the reading lives of children (and of adults too) which we want to set spinning in such a way that it goes on working when they are grown up. The circle looks like this:

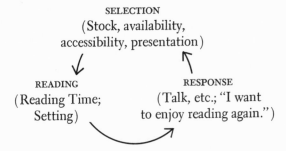

SELECTION
(Stock, availability,
accessibility, presentation)

READING
(Reading Time;
Setting)

RESPONSE
(Talk, etc.; "I want
to enjoy reading again.")

1. *Selection.* All reading begins with selection. You cannot read anything until you have decided what to read. How we make that decision is influenced by a great many factors. We shall be considering them in a later chapter. For now let us simply acknowledge the fact that selection is where reading begins. This means there must be plenty of books to select from, that they must be easily available, and that they can easily be borrowed or bought so that they may be read whenever and wherever the reader wishes.

2. *Reading.*   It is pointless spending time and effort selecting
something to read if we never read what we have selected. And
it is another fact of life that we cannot read anything, even the
shortest factual message, without time to read it.

Where works of literature are concerned, *time to read* is a
vital factor in the activity. You cannot get pleasure from a literary
book until you have "lived inside it" — have discovered the
patterns of event, of character, of language, of meaning, being
woven in it. Books for very young children are designed in
pictures and words that allow this "becoming the story" to take
place in one reading of only a few minutes' duration. But for a
very young child sustaining concentration for a few minutes —
five or ten — is demanding. And only when they have gone
through this experience a considerable number of times do they
begin to know exactly what is being asked of them and what
they must give in order to receive the pleasures that lie stored
between the covers of a book. Equally, this process of building
up pleasurable experience, and expanding the length of time a
person can give to each occasion, depends on a regular "giving of
oneself" to books.

So *time to read* is a major element in any intelligently
planned reading program for children in school.

Reading is also an antisocial activity. It is about the relationship between a reader and a book. Other people can get
in the way, can disturb that relationship. So can other people's
noise and sociable activity — television, gameplaying, conversation, domestic routines. So just as we need time to read, we need
places to read. We set aside places to sleep and cook and wash
and defecate. If reading is as important to our imaginative and
intellectual and emotional life as feeding and cleaning ourselves
are to our physical life, as I believe it is, then it deserves no less
in special provision of circumstances. Which means we must
create a *reading environment* that helps and encourages reading
rather than works against it. What that reading environment
requires we discuss in Part Two.

3. *Response.*   It is a fact of our psychology — of the way people
are made — that we cannot read anything without experiencing

some kind of response to it. We might be bored and fall asleep. But this is itself a response to what we are reading.

Literary reading can affect people in all sorts of ways. We will be sorting out some of the more important, as they relate to helping children grow into thoughtful readers, in later chapters. For now all we need note is that the most important response of all is the one that comes from our having enjoyed a book so much that we want to experience the same pleasure again. This may express itself as a desire to read the same book again, or to read more books by the same writer, or more books like the one we have just finished, or simply a desire to read again for the sake of the activity itself. The result, however, is that we are compelled to make another selection. The reading circle is completed and we set off again on a journey of literary discovery.

Many teachers and librarians, and parents too, are very good at encouraging children to select books. They spend considerable thought and effort on finding ways of stimulating children to want to read. Fewer adults, professional or not, are good at helping children find the time, the stamina, the concentrated energy to read what they have chosen. And fewer still are good at helping them in their responses to what they have read. And so the reading circle is often broken before the sustaining pleasures of reading are discovered. What we are discussing in this book are the staging posts around that circle where adults must be waiting and ready to intervene and help children, individually and in groups, to keep the circle turning.

THE READING ADULT

Right at the outset I made the point that readers are made by readers, and nonreaders are made by nonreaders. The role of the adults in children's reading lives cannot be overestimated in importance. Parents cannot complain, and neither can teachers, about children never reading anything, or anything "worthwhile," if the adults themselves are not seen to read, and to read with enjoyment.

What is more, we all of us — children and adults — try to

make other people into the kind of reader we are ourselves. If we have a strong liking, say, for detective stories set in the nineteenth century then, whether we are conscious of it or not, we will try to pass on our enthusiasm, will try to make reading allies. Of course, many of those we try to influence in this way will reject what we are offering. Quite often adults see this, when children do it, as a rejection of reading itself. But in most cases what is happening is that a child is rejecting only the selection he is being offered.

This means two things:

1. Teachers and librarians especially must, as part of their professional responsibility, make sure that their adult tastes are kept open and receptive to different kinds of story, different kinds of book, from the ones they naturally like. And they must be seen by children to read for their own adult sakes books which are "theirs," are adult, and not only children's books or professional studies. Yet of all the great number of courses and conferences about children and reading held every year how many include sessions on the reading those professional adults might do for themselves? How often are teachers and children's librarians helped in the way they are intended to help children — that is, to keep on growing and developing as readers of literature? To me it seems only professional common sense, to put it at its lowest, that every substantial meeting of teachers and children's librarians should include a component devoted to adult literature.

2. We can never entirely escape our prejudices. Children should therefore be dealt with by more than one professional who has an interest in reading. Storytelling and reading aloud, book choice and discussion sessions — whatever the activity, various adults should from time to time share the burden so that no one adult's tastes and prejudices dominate a child's reading life. How this can be done is suggested in the pages that follow.

THREE READING MOODS

In outlining the supposed "stages of development" in reading, I emphasized that these were never steadily passed through, that in fact they can coexist. We can be in various stages at once, and the "stage" which predominates is determined by what I call our reading "mood."

1. *Reading for the Familiar Past.*   In this mood we feel anxious, tired, lazy, worried — whatever causes us to reject demanding and "new" literature and forces us to take up again books that are comfortably — and comfortingly — known and easily enjoyed. Bedtime reading is often of this sort. And the classic example is the high school student who walks out of the library clutching a copy of Dickens or Jane Austen or George Eliot or some other text set for close study at school, and a copy of a Nancy Drew or Hardy Boys story that was first enjoyed years ago. Such combinations of choice, incongruous and sometimes even irritating and worrying to adults, are in fact an essential ingredient of all literary reading. We should never try to stop it happening, even though it can often be helpful professionally to know why a child is busy with the familiar past because knowing this can help us in the making of new choices.

2. *Reading for the Pertinent Present.*   In this mood we select books that connect with the way we are now, with the experiences of life we are presently encountering. It is the kind of reading people do when they are interested in what is happening to them and wanting to explore it as deeply as possible. And in my view it forms the basis of our reading as a whole. We relax from it or thrust ahead of it now and then but always return to this as the focal point of our reading lives. In a sense, until we have discovered ourselves and the way we are now in literature we find it hard to make lively connections with books that are about the less familiar or the otherness of life. This *literature of recognition* — and discovering what books work like this for individual children — occupies a fundamental place in any adult's work with young people.

    This explains why some books that were enormously important to us years ago seem, on rereading them now, to be quite astonishingly lacking in value. And why, on the other hand, we can reread a book after a gap of time and discover in it all sorts of connections and attractions it did not have before. We change; our experience of books between one time and another adds to the resources (of knowledge, skill, appreciation) we bring to a rereading.

We must also beware, as professionals dealing with children asking for "another book like this one," that the connections which have meant so much to the child are accurately identified. I remember a girl who asked why I hadn't more animal stories to offer her. When I asked for an example she said, "*Planet of the Apes*." Together we then worked out that what she really wanted was stories about the possibilities of animal-human relationships. O'Brien's *Mrs. Frisby and the Rats of NIMH* and some of the stories by writers like Ray Bradbury were closer to what she wanted than more conventionally obvious animal-stories would have been.

The connections books make with us, the reasons why they seem pertinent to us at one time and not at another, do not relate to such plain matters as their themes and subject-content being related in some direct and obvious way to our present needs. This is another reason why adults must learn much more about the fruitful ways of engaging children in talking about their responses to books, for only by such talk can we uncover the underlying and potent connections reading can make.

Let me give a vivid example. I once taught an academically "less able" and socially "disadvantaged" fourteen-year-old boy who stubbornly resisted reading anything other than the special interest magazine he devoured weekly. But one day he sat through class hardly taking his eyes from a fat-looking hardback book the pages of which were solid with unrelieved print. The book turned out to be the unabridged version of *Robinson Crusoe* which he had somehow come across himself and which he could not remember anyone ever having mentioned to him. He carried *Crusoe* about with him obsessively for weeks and seemed to read it whenever he got the chance. His progress was slow but dogged and he was clearly enjoying himself.

When he was near the end I talked with him about the book and discovered that the reason he liked it so much was that Crusoe was a loner, a man on his own, not just socially but physically, and surviving off the land in a primitive way. The book of course describes Crusoe's daily life in great detail.

All this, and especially the minute practical detail, was apparently riveting Terry's attention. And I knew why. He was a loner himself, a small-town country boy who spent most of his time wandering about the hills and fields near his home. School he loathed; he was by all the commonly used evidence just barely literate. When he read aloud the experience was painful both to him and his listeners. But yet Defoe's eighteenth century style, full of (for Terry) unfamiliar grammar and diction, not to mention long passages of (to me) tedious moralizing and philosophical musings, and not exactly well-stocked with dramatic excitements to relieve the steady pace, seemed not at all to put him off. Just the opposite. He defended the book vigorously as the only story he had ever read that was worth anything.

This was reading for Terry's pertinent present of a kind no one, I think, could possibly have predicted. And it reinforces again two crucial points. First, that we must provide children with a very wide range of book stocks from which to make their own selections. And that they must be given time to read what they have selected for themselves in an environment that makes it possible for them to attend to their reading without interruption or distraction.

One more point Terry's example shows up, not to do with the reading, but with the response to what we read. I have to admit that I doubt very much that Terry could have cared less whether or not I talked with him about Crusoe. But the fact that I did led to an interesting result. Though he began talking very reluctantly, we slowly shared what we knew of the story. As a result of that talk Terry later read the book again because, he said, he now realized he had missed a number of things I had mentioned and he wanted to read about them for himself. (The circle turning again.) But I did argue with myself for a while before having that conversation with him. It might have been the case that my attempt to find out what was going on would work against his pleasure and his private relationship with Defoe and Crusoe.

What is immediately pertinent to our lives is also most easily threatened or is itself threatening. So we are often careful to whom we talk about it, and about when we feel ready to talk.

Take an obvious case. Suppose an eleven-year-old's parents have just split up. The child may well read stories in which that event happens. *It's Not the End of the World* by Judy Blume, for example, or *The Pinballs* by Betsy Byars, or *The Runaway Summer* by Nina Bawden — or all three, obsessively reworking the experience in various story treatments. But talking about reading those books in the middle of a school class to a teacher who is not a confidant might be just the thing the child does not want just then. The books do not threaten or bully or tell anyone else about one's difficulty. But they allow one to contemplate the event in the security of the story.

We are happy to talk about books that belong to our past because they no longer threaten or confuse us; we talk heatedly about books that lie beyond our present concerns because these allow us to speculate, and often present us with puzzles we want to explore about the nature of being alive and "other" than we are. These we read when we are in the third "mood." But the books children read for their pertinent present they reveal, and adults should treat, with more caution and wariness. They touch on raw nerves.

3. *Reading for the Possible Future.* This is the mood that teachers most usually want to encourage. In it we feel a desire to explore books that carry us ahead of where we are now — where we are in our lives and as readers. They stretch and challenge us. In this mood we feel energetic and confident, willing to be subverted and changed. We are often at our most critically sharp and willing to discuss with other people our reactions and responses. It is the time when adults can, as Helen Gardner suggested they should, help children "to read with more enjoyment and understanding" what they, the adults, "have found to be of value."

For teachers the problem is that at any one time a group of children working together will be in various combinations of these moods. And when it comes to group work on a given text, therefore, the teacher's first job is to create a corporately responsive mood that helps most of the children (we never succeed with all of them at once) engage in appreciative activity.

PART TWO

The Reading Environment

V

The Set and the Setting

One day, quite a few years ago now, a middle-aged mother discovered that her teenage daughter sometimes smoked pot with her friends after school. Distressed, anxious, not a little angry, she at first decided to confront her daughter and put a stop to the affair at once, brooking no argument. On calmer reflection, however, she thought a more reasonable and reasoning approach would be better. After all, she told herself, what did she know about smoking pot? She had never experienced it, and expert opinion about the dangers and effects is contradictory. Besides, her daughter was sixteen, a child no longer; surely it would be better to talk the matter over and try and reach some kind of understanding?

That evening the girl made no bones about the fact that she used the drug, and during the ensuing conversation said again and again that without trying it no one could possibly appreciate the attractions. Very well, said the mother at last, in that case she would discover for herself. She proposed that after school next day the girls should come to the house and allow her to join them in smoking some pot. The daughter agreed and the meeting took place as planned with predictable results. This superficially admirable attempt at mutual understanding through shared experience (just what I shall advocate should happen in adult-and-child discussions of literature) was a complete flop.

Apart from the fact that cannabis often shows no appreciable effects the first time it is taken, two important factors in the situation were not helpful and made failure likely. First, the participants were in the wrong frame of mind to enjoy what was happening to them. And secondly, the surroundings were not conducive to the experience. The girls were wary, nervously self-conscious, quite unable to behave in a natural and relaxed way. The mother, a little afraid and expecting the worst, was unsettled, despite all her efforts to be open-minded, by her preconceptions not only about the drug but about the rights and wrongs of the position she had put herself into. And making matters worse, this uncomfortable group sat in a suburban sitting-room flooded with afternoon sunlight like dutifully polite guests at a formal coffee party. Not surprisingly, the girls went away embarrassed, and the mother, if she was any better informed, was certainly none the wiser.

The two factors which predetermined failure in this unhappy incident attend the outcome of every human activity, social and private, formal and informal, from lazy picnics during summer vacations to major crises at work. Borrowing terms from the psychologists, I call them the set and the setting.

By set I mean that mixture of mental and emotional attitudes people bring to the things they do: their expectations, previous experience and knowledge, present moods, relationships with other participants.

By setting I mean the physical surroundings in which the activity takes place and their appropriateness, or otherwise, to that activity.

Thus a picnic can be a disaster simply because one dominant member of the group is set against it — is feeling bloody-minded we might say — because he is there out of a sense of duty, rather dislikes the others, and generally cannot abide eating outside anyway. And no matter how set everyone is to have a good time, it is difficult to do more than make the cheerful best of things if the picnic is held, for some crazy reason, on a stinking garbage dump in pouring rain: the setting is not favorable.

On the other hand people passionately devoted to a hobby or sport or their work will endure without complaint conditions which less ardent folk think outrageously insupportable. So we see extraordinary hardships cheerfully borne (indeed, apparently enjoyed) by zealous mountaineers, earnest single-handed yachtsmen floating round the world, and all-weather fishing-hobbyists who weekend after weekend sit patiently at the side of, and sometimes in, rivers, undeterred by the paucity of their catches. Which leaves unmentioned the crowds of people who, because they are "on vacation," placidly accept treatment aand conditions they would reject as barbaric at all other times in their lives.

Set, it seems, is a more powerful influence than *setting*. But both play their part and in fact modify each other in forming our behavior.

Reading is no different in this respect from anything else. Come to it willingly, seeking many pleasures from books, and you soon find enjoyment. Have it foisted on you as a duty, a task to be put-up-with, from which you expect no delight, and it can appear a drab business gladly to be given up. Settle down somewhere pleasant and quiet and you can read for hours; do the same where numerous momentary distractions constantly interrupt your attention and even the most willing reader will feel like giving up after a short time. For me personally, the picture of myself in a dentist's waiting room is a perfect metaphor for a set and setting very much in play against the easily obtained pleasures I usually get from reading.

Obviously, then, anything we say about introducing books to children must always be accompanied by an understanding that the set of the teacher and children involved, and the setting in which they meet and work, will make their own contributions to the success of whatever methods are used. These two elements working together create what I have called *the reading environment*. Everything said in the rest of this book must be placed in this context.

THE SETTING

Two things must be carefully kept apart in our minds: The places where books can be found if and when children want them; and the conditions in which teachers introduce books to children.

About the first I have no doubts. The ideal — which we are laughably far from attaining — is that books should be spread with prodigal generosity throughout the community. Wherever people go there books should also be. This may sound like the pipe dream of a dyed-in-the-word fanatic. But surely it is no more than educational common sense when we are thinking about books in schools? Certainly the last thing we want is that books be shut up in tastefully decorated warehouses, watched over by highly trained storekeepers whose main purpose is to see that everything is kept tidily in its place and, as far as possible, untouched by human hands — especially the sticky-fingered hands of marauding children.

But what are the *minimal* provisions in the setting which every school ought to provide in order to encourage in its children (and its teachers) a desire to read, and facilities that make reading enjoyably possible?

1.   Collections of books should be sited and attractively presented in all work and leisure areas, not forgetting the staff room. These should always contain a proportion of literary work suited to the people who mainly use that area. For instance, the staff room library should at the very least include copies of books from which teachers frequently read aloud, a selection of the most important current children's literature and a "basic reference" shelf of books about children's books and reading.

2.   Some areas (note the plural), open at all times, should be made over and properly furnished specifically and only as reading areas for people who want to read undisturbed. The habit in elementary schools of organizing reading corners in classrooms might with benefit be adopted in high schools. By the way, if, as is often the case, these areas are defined by an arrangement of bookcases, which hold that room's library, the cases should be facing out from the reading area and not into it. People can then select books from the shelves without going inside the reading area and disturbing people using it.

3.   Book-promotional displays should occupy key sites in the building. Chapter seven deals with this in detail.

4.   There should be some arrangement for selling books, preferably through a school's own bookshop, no matter how primitive this is. Chapter ten deals with this.

5. It should go without saying these days that a school's own library ought to be active, inspirational, and central in the formal and informal life of pupils and staff. Librarians in charge ought to be at least the equivalent in every way — money, status, prestige, and administrative power — with heads of departments and subject faculties. Librarians should never be appointed as part of the administrative staff but always as part of the academic staff, for obvious reasons.

These seem to me to be the permanent features which are necessary in providing a background setting. When we come to the art of introducing books to particular children at particular times, however, and in places often arbitrarily specified by time-table needs, then fresh concerns arise, to which the following check list has always been for me a useful guide:

1. What kind of surroundings would best suit the book (or books) I have in mind and the methods I intend to use in introducing them? Clearly, for example, dramatic improvisation based on a story or poem needs space, whereas a storytelling session with a group of infant children can happen in a small area.

2. Will the session be formal or informal? Will the children be seated as an "audience" facing a "performer," or in a circle as a group, each member of which can participate? Will everyone be sufficiently comfortable to avoid shuffling and distraction but not so comfortable that sleep overtakes lively attention? Will I, the teacher, be able to see everyone? The aim is to find a grouping that promotes the plans we have in mind and does not hinder them.

3. What will the children be able to see when seated? What do I want them to see? Where is the main source of light? Windows are a trap, not just because whatever can be seen through them is a natural focus of attention, but because anyone who has to be looked at and is in front of them is hard to see, a strain on the eyes.

4. What is the temperature? Too much heat, like too much

cold, dulls the mind. If possible, regulate the temperature before the session begins. Is the room ventilated? School rooms soon become very stuffy.

5. How good are the acoustics? How much voice projection is needed to reach the person who will be furthest away? Are there "dead" spots? (I once worked in a school hall where, in the very center, a voice from the front, only a few feet away, sounded like a gabble no matter how loudly or softly spoken. There was also a spot from which, if you struck the floor with a hard rap of your heel, you could almost count the reverberations as the sound bounced from floor to ceiling to walls to floor. The building was a new one.) Is it best to group the children in one part of the room instead of others? Sometimes in large rooms some display stands (which have additional advantages, see 9 below) put up around the area to be used will help deaden echoes and create a more intimate atmosphere, as well as allowing you to speak more naturally and quietly.

6. How likely is the session to be interrupted? School services especially — medical people, guidance counselors, career advisors, and the like — now seem to have *carte-blanche* to take children from classes as and when they please. The worst interruptions of all, in my experience, come from those public address systems rigged in many schools in every room and used apparently without a second thought by administrative staff. When possible expected interruptions should either be planned for or prevented beforehand. If it is a usual irritation then the matter should be raised at staff conference. There is little more destructive of a well-planned and conducted lesson than interruption. The effect is the same as it would be on a theater performance if the manager came on stage during the play and asked for the owner of a car number. . . .

7. At what time of day will the session take place? And what is the weather like? Children's responses vary according to both. Very young children settle easily to storytelling before bed but are less well disposed just after getting up in the morning. Late in the afternoon on Friday needs a different approach from

early Monday morning in the way books can be handled. A chilly, rain-soaked day can make a class unpleasantly irritable by mid-afternoon. We cannot alter such conditions; rather they alter the approaches we make to children and what we expect of them.

8. What is the physical state of the books to be handled by the children? How familiar are they with the books? Bright new copies of an unknown book naturally excite more attention than old "readers" soiled from overuse.

9. What is the decorative state of the room? Will it help or hinder? What can be done, quickly and temporarily if this is the only way, to improve matters? Echoing classrooms with bare walls and stark rows of desks do little to encourage favorable sets of mind. Fortunately books are themselves attractive; they do furnish a room. Allied material is fairly easy to come by — posters, publishers' promotion displays, child-produced drawings and models, etc.* A stock of such things ready for immediate use is well worth keeping from year to year. Display stands of very light construction that can be prepared beforehand and taken to the site of a lesson at the last minute are fairly easily available these days.

None of this is just a matter of appearance, of convention and uniformity and putting on a good show. The more care we take

---

*For a nominal one-time fee, the Children's Book Council, Inc. will put subscribers on a mailing list to receive *The Calendar*, a twice-yearly brochure containing short articles by and about authors, illustrators, publishing, book-selling, and events of national interest in the children's book field; and also to receive twice-yearly materials brochures, cataloging book lists, and book marks, posters, and streamers designed by well-known artists, as well as materials available from publishers. The Council is headquarters for National Children's Book Week and a center for children's book promotion. It maintains a children's book examination and professional collection open to the public. For information on subscribing write: The Children's Book Council, Inc., 67 Irving Place, New York, N. Y. 10003 (Tel. 212/254/2666).
The National Book League, The Centre for Children's Books, at Book House, 45 East Hill, London SW18 2QZ (tel.: 01/870/9055/8) is a source of similar information in the U.K.

to prepare stimulating and book-focused surroundings which are appealing to work in the more effective we shall be.

THE SET

A child's set about books and reading may be deeply ingrained as a result of earlier reading experiences, or it may be temporary and changeable. We have already mentioned some of the factors that help to create ingrained sets but we must note them again.

1. Previous chapters have emphasized how early experiences with books and reading help create attitudes and expectations of a generalized kind. When these are favorable, a teacher can build on them with the child's cooperation. Otherwise there are barriers to be broken down before progress is made.

2. Disabling difficulties when learning to read can build antagonistic sets. These may come from poor teaching; frequent absence from school during this stage; physical disabilities of the eyes which are not diagnosed early enough; emotional disorders unrelated to reading itself but which cause difficulties; or learning problems posed by the many manifestations of dyslexia, even when diagnosed and under treatment.

3. Because, as I noted before, books are so much at the heart not of "education" but of "the process of education" — one of the essential tools — children quickly learn to regard them as symbols of everything bound up with school life. Then there are those children made to think themselves failures because of the hammer-blow terms like dull, backward, retarded, underprivileged, disadvantaged, handicapped, less able, slow, rejected, remedial, reluctant, disturbed — we have an armory of diminishing terms to apply which fool no one, least of all the children they label. Not unnaturally they snipe back by loading onto the symbol of their failure — books — all the things they resent, including their sense of inadequacy, and then reject as unnecessary to themselves and their desires everything associated with the symbol. Reading thus becomes an activity for intellectuals — for "clever people" — an elitist activity to be not just

ignored but attacked. A sixteen-year-old boy said to me on the day he left school, "I'd read a lot if I was clever, but I'm not, so it isn't worth the bother, is it?" In that one comment is hidden the tragic result of an induced attitude — the set — I am trying to describe. The spiral begins its downward swirl very early in life: a child has difficulty learning to read; this puts him back in his other school work, and because he falls behind he is labeled by a term of educational jargon verging on abuse, and this is dispiriting, makes him feel somehow deficient — and all because of his difficulty in making sense out of words in print with which his troubles began. Children in this state are in a crisis of confidence from which they must be relieved before their set about books can be refreshed and enlivened.

4. Children suffering from emotional or mental strains may lack the kind of concentration reading demands. The extreme form is seen in people who need medical aid. But there are milder forms. These are the periodic times of strain we regard as healthy and normal, like blue moods and fits of depression, or times of great excitement. The effects are the same but different in intensity and duration. First the desire to read is sapped, then the will, and finally stamina to tackle anything but short, and immediately useful, passages. Here again we have to remember the importance of knowing the children we teach well enough to understand what is happening and to be able to pin down the causes. It is frequently lack of such knowledge that causes teachers to accuse children of being lazy, un-cooperative, insubordinate, rude, or plain bananas, when even a slight investigation of their circumstances would reveal very good reasons for their behavior. Once we understand a child's prevailing set we are better equipped to decide on the strategy and tactics needed to change it. We can judge when to be firm and involved, when to leave alone for a while, when to insist and correct, when to employ this method or that. Without such knowledge we are rather like a doctor who treats symptoms only and acts on guesswork, inquiring neither into the cause of the ailment nor its history.

5. I have already gone into the adverse sets created by misuse

of books: the effects of monotony, drilling, meaningless drudgery passed off as "studying literature." And I have tried to suggest that the teaching of literature does not best proceed by exercises in tests of understanding, of vocabulary, and formal analysis of character, plot, structure, images, and so on. Not, at any rate, in the years up to sixteen or thereabouts.

Sets which become deep seated are not changed in a moment — neither the favorable nor the unfavorable. There is no formula prescription, no simple panacea which will revive damaged sensibilities quickly. This is something quite different, however, from momentary deviations from a consistent set. Children no less than adults are subject to fits of boredom, to times when they feel glum or restless when everything they usually enjoy lacks attraction, purpose or pleasure. Transitory circumstances of daily life are what cause these shifts.

The difficulty for teachers, whose work is in part determined by specified times when it must be done, is that they cannot just duck away when children, individually or corporately, are set against what is being asked of them. Indeed, many of the circumstances which create unfavorable sets are inherent in the conditions under which children are taught. We must therefore take into account this phenomenon and be prepared to tackle it.

We can group the most common unsettling influences under headings.

Physical surroundings (Setting)

These have been discussed in the first part of this chapter.

Conditions immediately beforehand

Children come into a lesson or a library visit from something else. What they have been doing, how they have been doing it, produce psychological states which show themselves in the "mood" they bring to the new activity. Coming from an exciting game on the sports field, for example, hardly dry from showering, children are often in an agitated frame of mind. They are chattery, still occupied with the game, perhaps not yet ready to engage at once in something that demands, say, silent and calm attention. Faced by this situation a teacher who launches into the presentation of a new book without first doing something to settle the children down and create a set ready for the book should hardly expect to succeed. Similarly, a class — or a child — that has been involved in a telling-off for any one of the myriad trivial transgressions their flesh is heir to, from talking too loudly in a corridor to baiting an incompetent member of staff, can arrive at the next lesson aggressively uncooperative or giggly. On the other hand, they can come from a well-taught science lesson as devoted to the search for scientific truth as a research professor and thus be so mentally and emotionally set upon that course, that any abrupt and unsympathetic attempt to switch them onto a track taking them in another direction will be as surely disastrous as would the sudden reversal of an express train. It can be quite as difficult to take over from a brilliant teacher as from an incompetent one.

Such examples could be listed endlessly. The point is that no session with children can be properly planned and begun without some thought being given to the prior events that have shaped the children's momentary sets. And this also means that a teacher must have enough skill and confidence to improvise when he discovers an unexpected "mood" in the children he meets.

Forthcoming events

Just as prior circumstances are dispositional, so are prospective ones. These may be regular and seasonal, like Christmas and school vacations, or occasional and minor, like sports matches. The onset of examinations, particularly important "public" exams which will determine the examinees' future, has a disturbing effect; and so does the approach of leaving school — upon graduation, dropping out, or even changing schools. Children involved in important school occasions (and important must be judged from the child's point of view not the adult's) are often not "themselves" beforehand — occasions like school play performances, orchestral and choir concerts. The arrival of the school doctor or dentist or of well-known personalities visiting the school — the catalogue is again endless, and we must plan as best we can for known events while contriving to improvise when, as often happens, such stirring distractions occur unannounced.

Adults' and peers' attitudes at particular times

These may be attitudes about current work — books being read, for example — or attitudes to the school generally. For example, senior classes who have grown into book-consciousness infect junior classes with some of their enthusiasm. Peers and adults who are admired, for whatever reasons, tend to be copied and followed, and a wise teacher will try to draw in to the book environment those adults and children who are opinion-makers and trend-setters.

Anticipation

This is a predisposing influence based upon past and present experience which makes people look forward to doing something, or the contrary. A skilled teacher can create a pleasant sense of anticipation, a desire to go to his sessions. One teacher I knew used to poke his head round the door just at the end of the day and say something like, "Tomorrow when we meet I am going to tell you about the evil magician . . . ," and then he would disappear leaving us all agog. Or a note would arrive at the end of a session to be read out to us: "Next time you join me in the library prepare to meet a ghost." We couldn't wait, of course. I do not recommend this as the only or the best way of creating expectations but it points in the right direction.

Comedians, heroes and villains

The comic butt, the natural-born leader, and the bully — representative, archetypal figures, patterns of which are to be found in most groups of children. I mention them here to remind us that there are personalities in any collection of people who are at one and the same time barometers, indicating the climate within the social group they tend to dominate, and weather-makers, determining the climate as the influencers I mentioned above. They are useful therefore as ways into the group and as indicators of what the group is ready for. Giving a natural-born leader a new book to read for himself will mean that, if he likes it, very soon other children in the group will be wanting to read it too. And this might be a better way to get them to do so than the teacher making direct approaches to them either individually or corporately. We need to use peer influences in creating a reading environment and a set favorable to books.

I have spoken in general of temporary sets in relation to group responses, but I hope it is obvious that individuals within groups experience sets peculiar to their personal conditions at certain times. Thus there is usually at least one child whose current set runs counter to the prevailing group set. A class may be keen, alert, contributive, except for one child who is withdrawn, distracted, unresponsive. He faces a teacher with a difficult problem: how far does one go in turning a blind eye, leaving him alone? Should a teacher *always* attempt to engage such a child's attention? Should he be firm and persistent? It is at this point that many factors come into play: the teacher's experience, judgment, knowledge of the child. There is no suitable generalization to be made, except perhaps to say that any attempt to coerce a response without good reason based on that child's present predicament is to place in jeopardy not only the child's willing engagement now and in the future, but also the prevailing favorable set and attention of the rest of the group. A lesson all teachers have to learn is that they cannot carry all children with them all the time. Nor is one session the be-all and end-all of their work or a child's progress. Literary readers are not made in a day, but grow and develop and mature over years. Nor is this growth, as we have said before, steadily progressive, like a car assembly line, bit being added after bit with smooth, robot efficiency. Rather, readers grow by fits and starts, now rushing ahead, now lying fallow, and now moving steadily on. In the day-to-day practice of their art it is easy for teachers to lose sight of this truth and think they personally are failing when all that is happening is that children follow perfectly natural, if erratic paths on the way to becoming adult.

VI

Browsing

Few pleasures, for the true reader, rival the pleasure of browsing unhurriedly among books: old books, new books, library books, other people's books, one's own books — it does not matter whose or where. Simply to be among books, glancing at one here, reading a page from one over there, enjoying them all as objects to be touched, looked at, even smelt, is a deep satisfaction. And often, very often, while browsing haphazardly, searching for nothing in particular, you pick up a volume that suddenly excites you, and you know that this one of all the others you *must* read. Those are great moments — and the books we come across like that are often the most memorable.

Bumping into books, as it were, has very little to do with other people and nothing at all to do with reviews, or lists of recommended books, or seeing "the film of the book," or publishers' publicity. Yet every reader knows how important it is as a way of coming across the books one most enjoys reading — and this is what leads me to wonder whether we do not sometimes try too hard to get children reading. Perhaps we ought to trust the books themselves more than we do. Too much talk about them can even drive people away. No matter how well we read aloud or do anything else to focus children's interest on particular books, unless they are given time to roam about unhindered among books of many kinds, left alone to choose for themselves, and to do what any avid adult reader does, then maybe we labor in vain.

Letting children loose among a good stock of books to follow their own whims and fancies for a few minutes every few days is one of the cornerstones on which a permanent interest is built. There are a number of advantages.

Familiarity, first of all. People from "non-book" homes feel
that bookshops and big public libraries are alien places. All those
shelves full of books are forbidding, daunting. Where do you
start? Of course, once you get used to it, you develop a nose for
sorting out what appeals to you. But there is no other way to
get used to it than by doing it. Browsing time provided in
school, when there is a teacher or librarian that the children
know well, who will help if necessary, and when their classmates are there too, is the only way many children will ever
become familiar with books en masse. Left to themselves, they
will rarely pluck up courage to try. This is the proper purpose of
the "library lesson."

Unfortunately, many teachers in the past have felt that
library lessons should be used only to teach about the library,
by which they meant instruction in how to use catalogues and
reference books, and so on. Worse still, others used the time
for book-based project work and provided no time at all for
children to browse. As a result library lessons came into disrepute
and even today authorities speak against them, arguing that the
proper thing is for the library to be open to everyone at all times
(which no one disagrees about) and for children to use it when
they find it necessary, but that library lessons ought not to be
specifically laid down in timetables. But what then happens is
that only the avid readers browse in their own time. Everyone
else comes there only when sent by a teacher to look up a reference or to get a book needed for some work. Libraries, in short,
become no more than resource centers, and books no more than
tools. But, as I said before, literature is not a tool, and a library
is more than a resource center.

Browsing is more than just a means of familiarization with
books, however. No true reader can be expected to grow on a
diet of prescribed texts only, regardless of how well chosen they
are. No one can be completely successful in selecting books for
someone else. Children, like the rest of us, need opportunities
to seek out for themselves the books that will satisfy their
immediate needs and suit their maturity and skill and personality.
Browsing times offer that chance.

Undoubtedly, working with children individually, one-to-one, is important. Browsing time provides opportunity for this to happen. While a group of children is looking through the stock the teacher can circulate among them, talking and suggesting, hearing what a child has to say about this book or that. The teacher can encourage, stimulate, discuss in a manner quite impossible when dealing with the group as a whole. Just as importantly, a child can be left alone to follow his own inclinations. The "pace" of teaching can be geared specifically to the child instead of to the group.

Nor is the teacher working alone during browsing times. In Chapter eight I explore peer influences and note the importance of the suggestions children make to each other. While poking about among books children naturally discuss those they have read, swopping responses, and so leading each other on. The teacher may have said nothing, but by providing the right setting and the kind of discipline which allows quiet talk about books the children have been helped to help each other.

In schools that run their own bookshop (see Chapter ten) browsing time can include buying as well as borrowing, adding another dimension to the activity. On any one occasion there will always be children who do not want to borrow or buy, but they are still learning to live with books and how to search out the ones that interest them.

Unsupported by any other teaching methods, browsing is not, of course, enough to make children into literate readers. The idea that all we have to do is surround children with books and everything else follows naturally is naive. It would be enough for some but by no means enough for all. On the other hand it is equally true that this kind of setting and activity is much more important than its casual, relaxed and apparently unstructured appearance makes it seem. It is essential. Every child should have the opportunity to browse among a wide-ranging selection of literature at least once a week, and preferably every day.

VII

Adult Recommendations

There is a trap that people professionally responsible for the literary education of children tend to fall into: the belief that there are certain books which children, whether they like them or not, must be made to plod through in a kind of literary pilgrimage. Such cultural asceticism replaces "ought" for "like." The young "ought" to read Dickens or Shakespeare or Twain or Whitman. But if they are made to do so without enjoying what they read, how far have we (and they) gone? How much nearer have we taken those young people towards the goal of true literacy? Not far, I think, and we may even have helped them take a step or two away from it.

The pleasure principle is the one that should guide the recommendations we make. We should be clear in our own minds which facets of a book we believe children will enjoy before we promote it. This does not mean we shall always be suggesting books that have only minimal and crude attractions that pander to the baser side of the young. Far from it. There are many and different pleasures to be had from literature. What we must have decided on each occasion is which pleasures we will encourage — which expectations we will raise — in a particular group of children, knowing that these are the ones the book in question will satisfy. To do this successfully demands certain things of the teacher.

It requires first of all and above all that we balance intelligently two areas of knowledge: intimate knowledge of the books available, children's and adults'; and intimate knowledge of the children to whom we are introducing the books we select. Knowledge of the books can only come from a conscientious reading of them for ourselves. This can never be complete. The difficulty is eased however by a judicious use of reviews, book-lists, authoritative surveys, and by sharing our knowledge with colleagues in staff conferences and locally and nationally organized gatherings.

Knowing the books is in itself not enough. Those we decide to offer children must find a response in them. And this means we must acquire an ability to read as though we were the children we teach so that we read on one level as they do, discovering what they will enjoy, while on another level we assess with our adult and professional experience how far a book will deepen literary awareness. A hard task, but one that gets easier with experience. Any reviewer has similar problems. He must read, so to speak, beyond his prejudices and personal tastes and be able to acknowledge the qualities in a piece of writing regardless of personal biases. I have myself a well-known dislike for his-torical fiction; it is a genre that on the whole gives me little pleasure. But I hope this does not prevent my recognizing the fine things in the work of, for example, Rosemary Sutcliff or Scott O'Dell or Erik Haugaard. And I would regard any attempt to sway children to my dislike as a form of cultural bullying as offensive in its own way as physical violence, not to say a betrayal of my responsibility as a teacher. Indeed, it is a professional duty to equip oneself sufficiently to be able to help a child along as a reader no matter what genre appeals to him, leading him from author to author, book to book, with enough sure-footed con-fidence that he is guided up the literary mountain and not left wandering in the viewless foothills because of one's own in-competence.

Apart from these, other considerations should be remem-bered. We must learn to judge the occasion before recommend-ing a book to children: its possibilities, "mood," atmosphere. We must be ready to be flexible in our work, seizing the moment when it is ripe for introducing a book, and altering our methods to suit. Classes of children can sometimes prove to be stubbornly set against having anything to do with book introductions, and it is better then to engage them in other activities rather than be doggedly determined to have one's own way and to go on in the face of their antagonism. At another time, the same classes may suddenly, for no apparent reason, be only too ready for such an occupation and then one needs (and here one's depth of knowledge comes in again) to be able to decide immediately which books to mention and how best in the circumstances to recommend them.

Whatever the situation, prepared for or unexpected, it is always too easy to overplay one's hand, praising a book so extravagantly, so effusively, that many children are put off. Uncritical gush is as repulsive as dry compulsion. A moderating honesty does no one any harm. All books have their flaws and it is just as wise to point these out as it is to draw attention to strengths and attractions, for children appreciate such integrity. Besides, when they find that their expectations have been time and again falsely raised they will react against teachers who mislead them. This is why it is best to let a book speak for itself as much as possible: a few comments followed by a brief but representative passage read aloud is better than a lot of talk about the book and how much one liked it, for then each child has a chance to size up the book for himself, letting his own antennae tell him whether it is something for him or not. Of course, there are times when all of us, children and adults, come across books that deeply please us, and then it is possible and right to express that great satisfaction; in this case the recommendation is credible because it is seen against a background of perhaps enthusiastic but certainly not indiscriminate praise.

METHODS

By-the-way conversation

As much can be done informally and outside the classroom as formally and inside in recommending books to children. In a few minutes before or after school, during outings and "educational visits," and in all the other social out-of-class situations, there are opportunities for suggesting books. These occasions have the advantage of being relaxed, and particularly of being individual exchanges: teacher to child instead of teacher to group. Then the approach and the choice of books can fit the needs, capabilities, tastes, background and history of the children involved. No mystique surrounds this means of bringing children and books together. Parents do precisely the same thing with their children, and people with each other, no matter what their ages. Though in the teacher's case it does mean that he is more watchful for opportunities and more aware of the reasons for his choice of recommendations. But the relationship should be just as natural. For I must strongly emphasize that I am not suggesting that teachers should be bibliographic bores, literary missionaries, who blurt out titles and press books on children at every possible moment. One must choose the time and the place just as astutely as one must choose the books to suggest.

Following up such conversations is important. When a child shows a genuine interest in a book mentioned to him, a copy should be put into his hands as soon afterwards as possible. Avid young readers will more often than not search out a copy for themselves; but the less avid, and especially those who find reading difficult, need the kind of encouragement a teacher can give by taking enough care not just to mention books but to obtain copies for them.

Nor should the matter rest there. After a while — enough time for the book to have been read — the child should be given a chance to talk about it. But again without this being pressed upon him if he prefers to say nothing. Equally, he should be allowed to dismiss a book summarily if that is all he feels it is worth. No one ought to be given the idea that these out-of-class encounters are simply curricula extension courses. When there is a give-and-take of opinion in which responses are honestly stated without imposition from the teacher, a continuing dialogue grows up between teacher and child as it does between two people sharing mutual interests, and so books are brought into the center of everyday life, which, as I have stressed, is a basic condition in the education of young readers.

Displays and exhibitions

Putting books on show is a way of making recommendations by, as it were, remote control. In the chapter on "Set and Setting" I mentioned the way displays can help in creating a book-focal backdrop to daily life. But they do more than that. One teacher can work closely with only a few children. In a large school he may never even pass the time of day with the majority. Furthermore, it is an unpleasant but undeniable fact that some children will always find a teacher unattractive for all sorts of reasons, rational and irrational. Displays are a device by which he can reach out to both sections of the school community: children he doesn't know and those who don't much want to know him. When well organized and presented, displays take comparatively little time and effort compared with the value of their effect.

Like every method of recommendation, displays depend on two main ingredients: selection from the vast number of possible titles; and attractive layout, so that people will take notice of the books and want to know more about them. The primary rule to keep in mind is that displays work through visual appeal. The books selected, the decorative backgrounds, the captions, and titles — all must make an immediate impact on the eye. So color, design, texture, shape need attention. It is no use throwing a few books together on a stand and hoping. Some thought, care and skill are essential. There are other things to be kept in mind too:

1. Choice of site. A display set up in a dark corner of a busy corridor will receive little notice until it is knocked over. Plenty of light, with a display spotlight if possible, should illuminate the exhibition (a number of inexpensive, safe little spotlights intended for the job are now on the market). There should be plenty of room for people to stand and look without obstructing passers-by. And the display should be placed in such a position that whatever surrounds it draws the eye to it, rather than distracts. Displays should be centerpieces: a matter of choice of site, and then of positioning within the site.

2. We can learn from good shopwindow displays and from the best museums about such matters as grouping of books shown, the number included (clutter is ugly; and overcrowding confuses the eye), the kind of materials to use for backgrounds, the use of space, different levels, and the massing of different shapes. Avoid anything tatty, botched-up and sloppily makeshift.

3. Initial impact is a key factor. This has two implications.

First, every display should include some feature which has an eye-catching effect, and other features which hold the eye once it is caught. There are, in other words, two dimensions in any good show.

Second, every display has a limited life span. Once it has become too familiar, people cease to notice it is there at all and its usefulness is finished. It should be dismantled just before that moment is reached. The life span varies according to the number of possible viewers, the site, and the complexity of the display. In a stable community like a school, judging when a display has reached its end is fairly easy; one simply keeps an eye on the number of times it is looked at and how much interest it generates. Once numbers and interest begin to flag then it is time to make a change.

4. Open displays (as opposed to those cased-in or out of touching range) need daily maintenance. Things get moved and displaced. Books tend to be taken away by those who cannot wait to read them. Decorations get marked and damaged. Soon what began as an immaculate, well-presented show looks tired.

5. Books on show ought to be available in copies for borrowing or buying, if possible. It is pointless to create interest if it is then allowed to evaporate because the books cannot be obtained. There is a correlation between length of time spent obtaining the book required and loss of interest.

6. A bit of pegboard with a few books hung precariously from wire hangers and the whole thing stuck on a wall is not good enough for a permanent display arrangement. Money is always short in schools, and exhibition stands are expensive. But commercial stands are not necessary. Very attractive settings can be put together out of all kinds of likely and unlikely objects. I have used the following as structures on which to mount displays. Units from a Jacob's ladder built into an interesting shape, covered with sacking and decorated appropriately. Packing cases used like building blocks and attractively covered and painted. Gym gear, grouped, and decorated with netting. Art-room draw-

ing tables and sketch boards. Metal- and woodwork-shop benches and materials. Tailor's dummies and stage platforms. Necessity mothers invention, and certainly invention in the presentation of books mothers surprised interest. There are few departments within a school which do not possess or cannot produce objects that can be used as basic stands or as decorations to set off books.

7. Similarly, every department in a school qualifies as a useful site for an exhibition. Naturally, one thinks of sports novels in the gym and biographies of scientists in the labs. But that is a superficial beginning. There is every reason for putting poetry in the gym and fantasy stories in the labs. But it is well to remember, whatever one does, that for any kind of display outside one's own domain the willing cooperation of the relevant members of staff is an essential first step.

8. There are many variations on themes for displays. Some of the more common are:

(i)   Collections of new books put out to inform people of their arrival and to create interest while new.

(ii) Books with a common denominator, such as novels about the sea, books about treasure-seeking, mystery stories, books by a single author, historical fiction about a particular event, period, etc., fiction and non-fiction about the same person, settings, etc.

(iii) In celebration of a topical occasion or an exploit in the news.

(iv) Books produced by one publisher, or in a series, or illustrated by the same artist.

(v)   Award-winning books.

(vi) Books of the film, TV and radio adaptations, etc. — usually put on when the dramatization is showing locally.

(vii) Books reviewed in school magazine, library notes, class wall-newspapers, or chosen by panels of children.

Apart from book exhibitions there is supplementary value in displays of book-related material: Photographs and brief biographies of authors. Originals and/or reproductions of illustrations and book jackets. Work by children inspired by their reading (drawings, stories, poems, models, reports of visits to book settings).

All these are internally organized projects. Larger exhibits brought in from outside, from public library schools departments, traveling collections, publishers' and booksellers' displays, require careful management and a special attempt to make them worth all the extra effort and often extra money they cost by ensuring as good an audience as possible. This is why many teachers link them with special occasions such as PTA meetings and visiting days. The quality and kind of displays — or the absence of them — in a school is an accurate indicator of the value and place books hold in it. Certainly, if setting matters as much as I have suggested, and if teachers seek to recommend by more than in-class methods, displays will be a constant feature of a school's life.

In-class methods

I should say, first of all, that displays, of course, have a place in classrooms as well as in the open areas of a school. Teachers, regardless of a specialism (if they have one), should see that part of the setting they create in their own teaching areas is given up to books. This is one of the indirect methods by which they make recommendations.

Another indirect method is through class libraries and book boxes. No classroom should be without a fairly wide-ranging stock of books for reading by children at set times and in those moments when they are between jobs: when they have finished a piece of work and are waiting for attention, or as an interlude before starting something new, as well as for borrowing to take home. These stocks should consist of reference works of the standard kind — dictionaries, handbooks, concise encyclopedias, some information books on topics being worked on at the time — and of a selection of literature. This last is best put together from selections made by the teacher and added to by the children so that there is a feeling of corporate responsibility and interest in it. Through it, of course, by the titles each decides to put in, the teacher is actually recommending books to the children, as the children are to each other.

This classroom collection can be reinforced by what are in effect different forms of book lists and these are intended to lead children to books they can get from the central school library or from the public library. For example:

1. Catalogue cards are kept in a "Try These" file drawer for pupils to consult when deciding on a book to read. Each card has written or typed on it a title, author, and brief annotation outlining plot, characters, and an indication of the kind of book — a blurb written by the teacher, or by a child who has read the book and suggested it, or both. The cards can be arranged by subjects or by author or by any system that seems best in the situation.

2. "Have you read these?" charts. These are large sheets of cardboard or strong paper, containing book titles and short "blurbs," presented attractively. The number of titles on each sheet need not be great. A number of sheets can be prepared and used in turn from a set which is carefully stored. The books selected can be organized just like displays by theme or subject, author or series, etc. And the sheets can be decorated with drawings, book jackets, children's comments about the titles included, photographs, etc.

3. Wall-newspapers, class magazines and the like, produced by the children, can include a teacher's contribution in the form of a kind of review column in which he writes about books his "readers" might enjoy. (The same method is useful in the wider context of the school magazine.)

Direct methods during class teaching time are most useful for focusing attention on particularly important books which a teacher especially wishes to encourage his children to read. These methods are simple in outline, but they demand sensitive handling in practice, as I've already indicated early in this chapter. The right set must be stimulated, and the relationship between teacher and taught must be receptive.

The most usual approach is for the teacher to show the chosen book to his class. A minute or two is spent outlining what it is about, though without giving away any details which would be best enjoyed when met for the first time in a full reading, such as twists in the plot, unexpected endings, and the like. The aim is to whet the appetite, not to satisfy it. An extract may be read aloud, illustrations shown, and, in order to provide points of comparison, reference made to other books of a similar kind which some or all of the pupils have read.

This may stimulate some children to talk about the extract or about their reading as a whole. Such an inclination ought to be encouraged because it leads to the kind of discussion that makes reading a socially shared experience as well as preparing the way for more formal work with literature. Once they have grown used to the method, children themselves can hold "review" sessions in small groups or as a class, telling each other about books they would like everyone to read, an approach further discussed in Chapter eight, "Friends and Peers."

Many teachers make this kind of lesson a regular part of their program with all classes. Others are less regular, preferring to do so only when they feel it is especially appropriate. I would not myself want a set time on the timetable, but I do think it of sufficient importance and value to make sure an occasion is found every few days for a session of "book swopping" discussion.

In another style of lesson, the book is approached through film clips, dramatizations on TV, or played on records or tapes made either commercially or by children who have prepared a "radio" script version as an in- or out-of-class project. Afterwards, these incidents, scenes, whole stories, poems or plays are discussed, the original source always to hand and available for children to borrow.

Mechanically produced performances of this kind have peculiar advantages. To start with, commercial films and recordings are made by people with professional resources not available to most teachers. Secondly, children seem to attend with a different kind of intensity to electronic pictures and sounds. Thirdly, the burden of stimulation is removed from the teacher's shoulders, giving a welcome respite. Everyone's personality and skills are limited and soon become familiar to people in contact with them every day. If no relief is given from them, this familiarity brings diminishing returns of interest unless the teacher is of unusual quality.

But there are basic details that need watching in the use of audio-visual aids, details which may seem based on common sense but which are also too often neglected. School classrooms are sometimes extraordinarily badly designed with poor acoustics, ineffective blackout facilities, and notoriously eccentric electrical outlets. Lessons that depend on a sensitive response to images — to literary language and imaginatively used pictures — are ruined when inefficient equipment goes wrong or works with only crude results: hissing amplifiers, hazy film and TV screens, and the like. It is therefore a point of wisdom to ensure beforehand, no matter what the assurances given by technicians who are responsible for maintenance, that everything is in the best possible working order. Volume levels should be set at the beginning of the proceedings when the children are present because acoustics change with temperature and the number of people in a room as well as with the placing of loudspeakers. Then again, children like to be able to see the source of noise if there is no accompanying picture, so that tape or record-player speakers should be visible from all parts of the room. Naturally, having everyone in a position to see a screen in comfort must also be ensured.

Introductory lessons of this sort may lead to close reading of books the children particularly enjoy — directed study led by the teacher. Indeed, some teachers use these methods to test out books which they would like to use as directed study texts, judging from the class's response the reception a book is likely to get in the more formal and lengthy curricula situation. In this way the lines between one approach and another blur, as they should, into a continuous, smooth program of enjoyable work.

Records of reading

The general trends in reading activity in a school and certainly in a class are fairly easy to monitor. There are clear signs that give away what is happening, like the amount and quality of conversation between staff and pupils and among the pupils themselves about books, the keenness shown for new books, the rate of exchange in the central and class libraries. Less easy to monitor with comprehensive accuracy is the progress of individual children. Every teacher has a fairly sure idea of the reading done by some pupils — the very keen and the very poor — and can guess at the diet of those in the middle ground. But this is not good enough to isolate in any reliable fashion the modulations of any one child's reading behavior. To achieve this we need some kind of records.

No record system which is practicable in relation to everything else a teacher must do in his working day will reveal all it would be useful to know; there are — thank goodness — areas of children's lives still private to themselves. School is by no means the only place where they acquire reading material. The best that records can do is to trace the effectiveness of the teacher's and the school's direct influence. Even so, this is not something to be dismissed lightly. Teachers who keep reading records find that the light they throw on their work compensates for the irksomeness of the administrative chore of keeping them up to date.

When borrowed books must be charged in and out — as in libraries — no matter how rudimentary the system, maintaining records is relatively easy, a matter simply of routine clerical work. Some teachers have complained, when I make this point, that the work involved is nevertheless too taxing on their time. And so it will be if they try and do everything themselves. But keeping the kind of records I have in mind is something senior pupils in primary and secondary schools are quite capable of doing, and laying responsibility for the task on them makes sound educational as well as administrative sense. For several years I kept records of every child's daily borrowing in a five hundred plus secondary school; I cannot say that, with pupil help, I found this part of my job much of a strain, and the system could quite easily have coped with a far larger number of children.

These records were kept in squared column teacher's record books. One double page lasted one class for a year. Down the side, the children's names were listed; across the top a column was allotted to each week of the school year, indicated by the week-ending date. Each main subject section of the library was given a letter symbol: "Y" was the fiction section, "D" the history section, etc. This made for simplification of the entries. Each time a book was borrowed the relevant symbol was entered in the record against the borrower's name and in the appropriate date column. This chore was done at the end of the day by the pupil-librarian on duty, who used the changing cards handed in by the borrower to get the necessary information. Thus, part of one page appears in the records like this:

Form: 2C																
1962-63	←Sept→			←Oct			→		← Nov				→	←Dec→		
Wkd	14	21	28	5	12	19	26		2	9	16	23	30	7	14	16
Blanch, Susan				Y	Y	Y	Y		Y		Y	Y			Y	
Davis, Howard					Y	Y	C	Half term		Y	Y	S			Y	
Day, Jennifer				Y	Y	Y			Y	Y		Y				
Hathaway, Stephen							Y									
Hollywell, Susan				Y	Y	Y	YY		Y	Y	Y	Y			YS	
Lugg, Terry					M		Y		M			Y			M	

FIG. 1

Certain information is at once clear to anyone, even those who do not know the local conditions at that time. There are, for instance, three school weeks gone before anyone in this class of twelve-year-olds borrows anything. But once activity begins, Susan Blanch is a fairly steady customer, taking only fiction books, the section favored by most of the pupils (only a selection of children are shown in Fig. 1, of course). Terry Lugg, on the other hand, is a much less active borrower, though more active than Stephen Hathaway, and takes books from the science collection, the pure sciences at that (M). Susan Hollywell, the most frequent borrower of all, on two occasions (26 October, and 14 December) takes two books a week, one time taking, unusually, something from the fine arts section. It is noticeable too that these double borrowings occur just before holidays (half term and the end of term) which suggests she plans her reading.

Two years later when they were fifteen and on the verge of leaving school their records looked like this:

Form:4C														
1964-65	◄—Sept—►			◄— Oct				—►	◄—Nov—			►	◄—Dec—►	
Wkd	11	18	25	2	9	16	23	30	6	13	20	27	4	11
Blanch, Susan	Y	F		F	F	YY	Y	Y	JY		JJ		Y	J
Davis, Howard	X	S	D				X			Y	JS	F		
Day, Jennifer	F	S	F		YDF	XD	FX	JX		D		FF	F	F
Hathaway, Stephen		YY		Y	YS						Y			
Hollywell, Susan		YRY	X	RY	RYY	FR	RR YJ	YRY	FR RYR	RRJ	FRJ	YYJ	RF JF	YJ
Lugg, Terry	M	R		Y				M	S		Y	Y	Y	

FIG. 2

N.B. *Half term vacation fell in part of a week, so that it does not show in the records, as there was borrowing activity in the same week.*

Here again we get some interesting insights into these children which would not have been so clear without the records. Overall, the borrowing activity has increased considerably over the two years; and this time it begins immediately term opens. Susan Blanch has grown into a steady, totally fiction borrower who still finds a lot of books in the stock supplied by the school ("Y") but has begun to draw also from children's books ("J") and adult books ("F") supplied by the school library service. Jennifer Day selects almost completely from adult collections and has taken also some history and "Fine Arts" books. Susan Hollywell, of course, shows up as the outstanding person. (I remember her well, a plump, comfortable and invariably cheerful girl, and the kind of voracious reader you don't need records to tell you about — though they are useful as a graph of her choices.) She is still very much a children's book borrower, though there are some adult books in her selection ("X," and "F") with a smattering of titles taken from the applied sciences, which in Susan's case meant books on cookery and needlework. Stephen Hathaway is the problem child. He began his last year well enough, but as the year wore on and graduation day loomed up he became less interested than usual in anything to do with school. Stephen was a boy who found reading difficult, and no one ever quite managed to get him further than functional literacy.

There is in both sets of records a strong contrast between boys and girls, the girls being the regular and frequent borrowers taking mostly fiction and the boys being erratic and borrowing more nonfiction.

Overall these records were intended to reveal, and did, a number of factors:

1. The borrowing pattern for each child.
2. The borrowing pattern for the whole school.
3. The progress of the whole school and of individual children as the years passed.
4. The use made of the various main sections in the library.
5. The trends of boys' and girls' borrowing habits and preferences, and the contrast between them.
6. The classes where borrowing activity seemed below average, as a guide to where encouragement was especially needed.

Apart from such uses, however, records of this kind are valuable in suggesting approaches to individual children most in need of help. Stephen Hathaway is a perfect example.

Other kinds of records often employed are:

1. Reading diaries kept by children themselves. They write down title and author and perhaps a short comment against the date when a book was finished.
2. A list of titles and authors of books borrowed from class libraries, book boxes, etc., which the teacher keeps, allotting one page of a notebook to each child.
3. A list of books in the class collection, kept in a squared mark book. The children tick off the square under their name and in line with the relevant title when they have read a book.

These devices all have their advantages and disadvantages. When children are aware that records are kept there are always some who will want to impress or please and who therefore submit false reports, or borrow but never read what they borrow while pretending they have. Indeed, all records are subject to this weakness. They record what was taken, not necessarily what was read. Care must be exercised in seeing that these teaching aids do not become weapons to browbeat with: "I see, Johnny, that you haven't borrowed a book for weeks. Look at all these dreadful, empty squares! Now Sylvia has lots of entries under her name." This sort of competitive blackmail does nothing but worsen the problems that hinder poor readers and feed the egos of those held up for praise. Records should not be literary means tests and are best kept for background guidance only.

Furthermore, no record of borrowing or of "personal reading" based on books supplied by the school is ever a full account of all a child has actually read. Every child has a reading network, a complex variety of sources from which reading is drawn for many different needs. Children get books from public libraries, buy them from shops, borrow them from friends, are given them as presents. Magazines, newspapers, comic books — by many children these are more the source of their everyday reading than books themselves.

From time to time it is worthwhile for teachers to build up a profile of their pupils' reading habits by asking them to answer the following questions on a slip of paper:

1. List the newspapers you have looked at and read during the last week. Which parts did you actually read, rather than just look at?
2. Do you read these newspapers regularly?
3. List the magazines and comic books you have read during the week. Do you read them regularly?
4. Write down the titles of all the books you have read in the last two weeks no matter where you got them from.
5. Write down anything else you remember reading during the last week which you have not so far mentioned.

(It is rarely useful to ask for lists of book titles read in a period of less than two weeks, hence the nature of question 4. Some children cannot get through a longer story or novel in less time. If nothing is being completed in a two-week period then obviously the teacher needs to intervene and discover something about the reasons why — though without making this inquiry a threatening checkup.)

Such a questionnaire may not be strictly scientific and its results will be of only local and temporary use. But linked to the teacher's personal knowledge of the children involved, and the circumstances surrounding their work, this kind of profile reveals reading patterns and is of great help in making connections between the children's spontaneous interests and knowledge and the approaches made in teaching.

A final note to end this chapter. No teacher needs to, or ought to, work alone in recommending books to children. There are others who can be brought in, either to advise the teacher or to work with the children — for example, joining with other members of staff in promoting books among each other's pupils. But there are outsiders who can be brought in as guests — authors, illustrators, public librarians, booksellers, publishers, parents — anyone whose presence and refreshing unfamiliarity and enthusiasm for reading can help change the pace of everyday encounters between teacher and taught, and can show by what they say and do that literature and reading have a central and important place in our lives. I have called these guests "Star performers" and examine their contribution and the way teachers can organize visits in Chapter eleven.

VIII

Friends and Peers

No one needs to be told that children wield powerful persuasive influences upon each other. The fact that they do is not only observable every day, it is part of everyone's childhood experience. The friends children make, the peer groups they belong to — whether the Boy Scouts, the neighborhood gang, or simply a loose association of acquaintances who do things together now and again — have one result that matters in the context of this book. By a kind of fission process, a chain reaction, the young pass on from one to another their enthusiasms and concerns, their attitudes, interests and modes of behavior. How can we put some of this fission energy to work on behalf of children's reading? How can we channel it so that children help each other through the network of social relationships which so much affect their likes and dislikes, their disposition to engage in activities which are approved of and enjoyed by their contemporaries?

There are some techniques we can use that propel us in the right direction, provided that we have first of all created a set and setting (see Chapter five) favorable for them to work in. On their own, none of these techniques gets very far. But as part of a much larger program they add a dimension that cannot be achieved in any other way. For what we are trying to do through them is to make reading an activity promoted by children among themselves, in the same way that they promote among themselves interests in, for example, certain games, fashions of clothes and music.

"HAVE YOU READ THIS?" SESSIONS

These are times when children share their opinions about books they have read, recommending them to others. They can be organized in different ways, but the twofold effects are the same. The discussions make reading (which tends to be a private pleasure) into a social activity. And particular books are mentioned which others might be led to read for themselves.

The sessions may come about spontaneously: Gail mentions to her teacher that she has just finished a book she very much enjoyed; she is asked there and then to tell the others about it. Or they may be set times, prepared for beforehand by teacher and pupils, each of whom decides on the books to be talked about and what to say about them. Then in small groups or as a whole class together the children take it in turn to make their recommendations, conducting afterwards a discussion to which anyone who wants can contribute comments. Copies of the books mentioned are shown around, and are borrowed by those who feel they would like to read them.

However the sessions come about, the teacher has a sensitive problem in judging how much to take part: when to stay out of the discussion and when to have his say, when to guide and challenge and when to let the conversation follow its own path unhindered. He will be particularly employed, of course, as a chairperson, seeing that the floor is not hogged by a few articulate public speakers. And he can perhaps best contribute by feeding into the discussions references drawn from his wider reading experience and book-knowledge, helping to add depth and range to what is said and recommended. The unhappy tendency among teachers — an occupational neurosis — is to jump in too early and too often, especially if the talk wanders from direct comments about books under consideration, as though they have not realized that, except for carefully prepared debate, all talk now and then wanders down byways, for a moment or two, during which the participants gather themselves for a fresh attack on the main subject. It may sometimes be necessary for a teacher to bring a discussion back to the work in hand when it gets lost in a maze of trivia. But to prevent any meandering at all, or to dam the flow of talk too soon and too often by intruding, generally only frustrates the spontaneity wherein lies the pleasure and the educative value of this activity.

Certainly, at the end of these prepared sessions the teacher should consolidate what has been said in order to focus attention on the primary purpose of the technique: getting children to read books. ("John's group discussed *Jacob Two-Two Meets the Hooded Fang* by Mordecai Richler," he may say, holding up a copy. "John said he thought the story much more amusing than he had expected it would be. Susan's group looked at *The Borrowers* by Mary Norton . . . during which Helen mentioned how much she enjoyed reading *Charlotte's Web* by E. B. White," and so on. Thus making the dialogue straightforward as a summary of what was mentioned by the children.)

Variations can be built on this basic idea. A book-panel composed of members of one class can tape a discussion for playing to another class in the same age year: a kind of radio or TV book review program. Readings of extracts prepared by other children can help to exemplify what is said, and the choosing of relevant passages involves a class in considerable, but purposeful, literary criticism. A senior group may do the same sort of program about books they remember with pleasure from the time when they were, say, eleven, and the tape can be played to children of that age. This sort of approach can be used between schools who share each other's tapes. Alternatively the program can be given "live" before an "audience" who then add their own comments to the things said by the "panel." Again, this can go on between classes, between years in one school, and between schools of similar or different kinds.

Another method is to put children into small groups and leave them alone to talk about a book they have read. Recordings made of such sessions reveal how little idle chatter goes on, and how excited in a controlled way the exchanges become. Success partly depends on a teacher's skill in putting together compatible children, as well as on the care taken in preparing everyone for what is going to happen.

In my view, the mutual sharing of reading experiences through conversation of these kinds is the best method of all by which peer influences can be organized and channeled. As a child said to her teacher during a discussion about reading: "When books are recommended by your own age group you tend to go for those rather than the ones a teacher would recommend."

BOOK REVIEWS

As drill exercises in writing, or as a check that children have actually read what they say they have read, the writing of book reviews has little to commend it. Their only proper purpose is that they shall be read by others. Having made this prefatory warning, it has also to be said that many teachers successfully contrive to make reviewing an enjoyable and useful ingredient in their book and reading programs. The key to their success is publication. Reviews must be made available to their authors' peers. An obvious outlet is the wall-newspaper, another is the school magazine. Some teachers keep a library or class journal devoted to "literary magazine" material (reviews, stories, poems, articles about books, etc.). And there is the Review Folder: a loose-leaf file into which specially good reviews are put for permanent keeping and use. Any child who wants help in choosing a book is allowed to read through the folder to see if it suggests anything to him.

Anyone who has written reviews professionally knows how difficult it is to do the job well. Even in the basic form of bibliographic details, outline of content, response to content, and evaluation and comparison against other books of similar kind, a review is a very formal and structured essay. To infuse into that basic form an element of linguistic liveliness and wit, which marks out the best adult reviewers, is to ask far more than most children can hope to achieve. And so it seems to me that reviews we ask children to write should not be rigid in form. In many cases they may be no more than a short comment. Certainly by the age of ten or eleven children should understand what a good conventional review is like; but it is not necessary for them to be able to write one before their written comments on books can be used with their peers.

Again, there are variations. Some teachers put into the backs of books in their class libraries slips of paper on which children may write short comments. Others use instead a review catalogue: a drawer of catalogue cards, each bearing the book's title and author, on which comments can be written. Or a large sheet of lined paper is put up on the wall, and children can write things on it under the appropriate title. These methods are particularly useful with younger children who are not yet able to write long passages.

One of the most effective pupil-centered devices I have come across — effective because it stimulated other children to read what was recommended — was a Book Graffiti Board. A long notice board in a high school corridor was left free for any pupil to pin onto it anything at all that drew attention to a book the pupil had enjoyed and wanted to recommend. So much was it used that the board had to be cleared every two weeks. What was pinned up ranged from sheets of paper with nothing more written on them than a title and author to elaborate and beautifully executed illustrations, longish book reviews either typed or handwritten, and cartoons that made a joke about the book being suggested.

MAGAZINES

These may be ephemeral, like wall-newspapers, or more permanent, like the school magazine. They are less limited than review slips or files in that different approaches can be allowed: poems, short stories, brief biographies about authors, illustrations of scenes or characters, accounts of visits to places described in stories. In this kind of work, everything is book-based and may be tangential in recommending books to children, but frequently it is the effect a book has had on someone else that leads us to read it, rather than anything said about the book itself.

SELECTION PANELS

Every chance should be taken of involving children in choosing books intended for them to read: in class and school libraries, for sale in school bookshops, and for displays and exhibitions.

The act of reaching decisions requires discussion, sharing

of opinions, suggestions, and, of course, books to be read. If the panel members represent class groups, they must canvass for suggestions. If an entire group is involved, debate can be formally organized and kept going informally out of class by the teacher asking individual children their opinions. This kind of activity especially promotes controversy: there is competition to get one's own title into the final list. Children find themselves taking sides about what they have read or want to read and — the important thing — having to justify their choices.

If they are allowed, however, these selection methods must genuinely be what they claim to be, and not simply a front behind which the teacher does as he likes regardless of what the children decide. He can, after all, draw the limits, retaining for himself the right to veto or to select a certain proportion of the stock on his own. But the limitations set must be clearly defined before the panels go to work. And certainly, before selection meetings, there should be ample time for the children to argue among themselves. It is useful if exhibitions can be mounted or visits made to the public library or bookshops where a range of titles can be seen and browsed through. Children as much as adults need to make informed suggestions in book selection.

When all these techniques have been accepted and enjoyed, some critical questions that demand discussion will arise. How do you judge a book? What are you looking for when selecting for other people? What language helps you to make your thoughts about books clear? Are some books better than others? In what ways? How do you know? What is it you get from reading a work of literature? Are there different ways of reading? What are they? When such questions crop up naturally children are well on the road towards becoming literate readers. And their teachers can begin to make them aware of what is happening. Ideally, this point will be reached by eleven years of age, which means that steady work of the kind I've been describing must be carried on through the school years before then.

So these apparently superficial and peripheral activities, practiced in tandem with techniques outlined elsewhere in this book, lead directly to three centrally important elements in the making of literary readers: a vital social atmosphere that creates individual reading interests; the widening and deepening of children's own reading; and the articulation of responses — what in other contexts we would call criticism.

To these classroom methods, we can add two out-of-class features that lead in the same direction.

PUPIL ORGANIZERS

When people, no matter what their age, are involved in the organization of affairs, and especially when they have responsibility for at least part of the organization, their involvement, their commitment, tends to be greater, keener, than otherwise, and they tend to proselytize. In every school, from kindergarten onwards, there are opportunities for children to help with the organization and provision of books: in class and central libraries, in specialist collections, in putting on displays and exhibitions, in ordering and preparing stocks, in running the bookshop, in promotion and publicity, and the like. One example will demonstrate the potential — the minimum potential — for this kind of involvement.

A high school of five hundred boys and girls with a central library stock of 6,000 volumes and a number of class and specialist libraries under its wing provided opportunities for the following pupil staff:

    2 "senior librarians";

  15 "school librarians";

  40 "class librarians" — two a class;

    6 "specialist librarians" looking after collections in the science department, craft department, and main English room.

Their jobs divided up like this: of the fifteen school librarians, two seniors were in charge (one boy, one girl). Their duties as listed in the duplicated handbook issued to each pupil-librarian were:

1. To supervise the librarians.

2. To arrange duty rosters.

3. To make up the records daily (i.e. of books issued, etc.)
4. To come in before school each morning and check:
   (a) that the book checking system was in order.
   (b) that the library was tidy and presentable.
5. To check on overdue books.
6. To see that work was prepared for the duty pupil-librarian to do during recess and lunchtime.
7. To arrange for the decoration of the library: e.g. flowers, displays, etc.
8. To check daily with the teacher-librarian that all was in order and to receive instructions.
9. To arrange for and conduct library staff meetings weekly.
10. To train and examine pupil-librarians during their probationary period.
11. To liaise with and supervise class and specialist librarians.

This represents a considerable work load and requires a good deal of thought, time and energy from young people. But that was intentional. Because so much was demanded, as much was given: the job was worth having. Naturally, there were lapses and mistakes, and senior librarians varied in quality. But all of them did their utmost and knew that their position was a key one within the school.

The ordinary "school librarians" began their work at thirteen and could remain on the staff until they left school. They took turns in supervising the library in and out of school hours. In pairs, they looked after the condition of one section of the stock or had other areas of responsibility under the seniors. Everything, in fact, including discipline within the library was looked after by these young people.

The class and specialist librarians did with their smaller collections precisely what the school librarians did with the central collection, and attended the weekly staff meetings. They also knew the system in the central library so well that when their classes were in the main library they could answer routine administrative questions.

The educational potentials of such a system are obvious. Its pertinence here is that it infiltrates the school with a peer group and individuals whose concerns for books are practical, of daily importance. Their influence on the set and setting of the rest of the school reaches into every class, every curricular department. They are a leaven, helping other children by talking about books in an enthusiastic way.

Clearly, younger children would be unable to cope with the whole range of responsibilities and jobs borne by these adolescents; but there is still plenty they can do, even if under closer teacher supervision, with the same results. No matter how sophisticatedly professional and adult is the organization of school book stocks, or, at the other extreme, how young the children, it is, in my view, negligence of the worst kind to shut out pupils from an organization that is intended to benefit them and to help create in them a book consciousness. The emphasis should always be on the use of book stocks as an instrument to develop literary skills and the promotion of reading, rather than on bibliographic and library niceties that suit higher academic research more than they encourage a book-loving body of children. (See Chapter ten on book ownership for the place of the school bookshop in this scheme.)

BOOK CLUBS

Some teachers argue against book clubs, claiming that they bring together only a certain kind of avid reader, the literary equivalent of the religiously effete and over-pious. It is a danger; but it ought also to be said that school clubs invariably reflect the style and manner of the teachers who run them. Book clubs do not have to be cliquish, pretentious, stuffily self-inflated, or bolt-holes for ethereal literary spirits. On the straightforward point that they bring together only avid readers, it seems to me of great importance that children who are keen readers should have a chance to meet together. We do not regard such a thing as at all odd when hobbyists meet; rather, we encourage it. Bookish children, as they tend somewhat negatively to be called, deserve at least as much nurturing.

That apart, book clubs need not be enclosed, much less ingrown. One of their aims ought to be to mount open meetings which will attract nonmembers. A club should be a hub at the center of all the book-based activities involving the rest of the school. And the atmosphere, especially in elementary schools, should be celebratory, the events more akin to a literary workshop than to an adult lecture course. Talks on this and that aspect of books are all very well, but they can be overdone. Things like the following should be included on the program:

    play-making;
    writing and illustrating stories, poems, etc.;
    magazine production for class or school;
    book-related film shows;
    visits to exhibitions;
    storytelling and reading performances;
    model-making on book-related topics.

Obviously a great deal depends on the age of the children and their circumstances. But the aim is to create another cell within the body of the school, in this case composed of readers who are sustained by the club meetings and who establish a social book-center. Like the librarians and the bookshop staff, the club members are catalysts who spark off that fission which will spread from child to child an awareness of books and the habit of reading them.

IX

Worrying about the Rubbish

By "rubbish" adults usually mean literature which in their judgment lacks any artistic, moral or educational value. The objection to it seems to be that by reading rubbish children cripple their own imaginative, linguistic or moral powers, as well as their ability to come to grips with and appreciate good quality literature. Whatever the objections may be, one thing is sure: teachers and librarians worry about the rubbish children read. Their worries are not altogether unfounded but they are sometimes carried too far. No one would suggest that children should be encouraged to read rubbish — they do not need encouragement on that score — but some people would suggest that they should be strongly *discouraged*, and then, I believe, more harm than good is done. Let me try and give my reasons.

First of all, Dr. Johnson's well-known dictum is appropriate: "I would let [a child] first read any English book which happens to engage his attention; because you have done a great deal when you have brought him to have entertainment from a book. He'll get better books afterwards."* This matches up with what Helen Gardner says in the passage quoted where she recommends that the young need on the one hand "to be encouraged to read for themselves, widely, voraciously, and indiscriminately . . ." The teacher's job is to lead, to help children read "with more enjoyment and understanding what [they] have found to be of value." But this is not done by restriction, suppression or a snobbish dismissal of the "rubbish" that children happen to like. Even when a child seems to be reading nothing else but rubbish, at least we know that he is reading something: he still has a finger-

*Quoted in Boswell, the *Life of Johnson* for 1779.

hold on the written word, and we still have a hope of widening his range and vision. In the end, it is always better that children read something than that they read nothing at all.

But the problem is not usually so extreme. When children read at all they usually read more than a diet of rubbish only. (The only really worrying problem is when they read nothing.) And this introduces a second point. I am not convinced that people become "fans" or even connoisseurs — experts: educated and discriminating people in any sphere — from limited knowledge and experience, no matter how rich in quality. On the contrary, they are connoisseurs because they know their subject inside out: the good, bad and indifferent. Wide, voracious, *indiscriminate* reading is the base soil from which discrimination and taste eventually grow. Indeed, if those of us who are avid and committed readers examine our reading history during our childhood and look also at what we have read over the last few months, few of us will be able to say honestly that we have always lived only on the high peaks of literature. Nor would we have it any different. The sum total of the pleasure we have had from books owes something to the ephemeral, transitory material we have frequently read. There is no reason why we should think that what is true for ourselves will be any the less true in this respect for other people — children or adults.

Both the points I have made so far can be summed up in one: children must be allowed to discover for themselves. In the chapters on browsing and undirected reading I emphasize the fact known to us all that the books we come across by accident for ourselves often seem charged with greater attraction than those we are led to by other people. Inevitably, a large proportion of these self-chosen books will be slight in literary stature. But this is not what matters. The important thing is that by finding books in this unimposed manner we learn, however crudely at first, to compare, assess, select. There is no way this can be taught without direct, if haphazard, experience.

A third point, and one that harks back to the chapter on peer influences. Children have a group, social life; they belong to a clan of friends. And like any group, any clan, a company of children is cemented together by shared interests, which we frequently recognize as "crazes." For a time a gang of children may be consumed by an interest in certain comics, or motorcycle magazines, or pony books or stories about actresses or teenage romances. A parent or teacher who attempts to deny this kind of rubbish to a child is attacking the child's feeling of group identity, of belonging. And there is no sense in doing that. By imposing a ban one is only likely to set up antagonism and frustration which will turn against the very thing we are trying to encourage. This is not to say we should pay no attention to the reading children do as part of their group alliances. On the contrary, we can discover a lot from knowing about it. It can help us decide how to approach our teaching: the books we select and the techniques used to introduce and study them. Furthermore, children can be misled by group influences into reading truly pernicious material (hard core pornography, for example) and when this happens adults have a clear responsibility to step in and do something about it. But I'm not discussing pernicious material here. Rubbish is neither pernicious nor particularly enlightening; it is merely absent of literary quality. But even if I were to bring this aspect into view I hope we would want to agree that the way not to handle the problem is by an act of unreasoned censorship exercised with authoritarian zeal.

Reading crazes pass through groups of children like emetics, just as crazes for certain seasonal pastimes do. The interest is not really in the craze itself but in the intense, socially binding effect it has on the individuals in the group. What remains afterwards for the participants as individuals is a more or less (depending on the child) increased facility in the imaginative, mental or physical skills involved. Thus in games, manipulatory skills are often exercised and extended, as for example in games that involve running, climbing or making objects — bows and arrows, catapults, clothes for dolls, and so on. In reading crazes a child is exercising at the very least his ability to read; his reading muscles are limbered. And this is not to be dismissed lightly because it is an essential part of everyone's development as a reader. What is more, when a number of children read the same book with the kind of intensity they do during a craze, they talk and argue about it with equal intensity and so are forced to explore their individual and group responses, to formulate and articulate their enjoyment or dislike. They become involved, in other words, in criticism. In the beginning it does not matter what kind of literature causes this to happen; the great thing is that the critical sense has been awakened.

We are drawn back again — and this is the fourth thread in my argument — to my earlier assertion that what should concern us most is how and why children read, not what they read. I am not at all persuaded that children read everything in the same way, any more than adults do. Just the opposite. It has been frequently noted by writers on this subject that all children seem to find a source of security and comfort in certain kinds of books. Usually these are books which are very familiar to them, or are by a writer of whom they are fond. At other times they may be doing nothing else but relax: passing the time in a pleasant if untaxing recreation. More often than not books chosen for this kind of reading are, in adult eyes, rubbish. But to tamper at such times by trying to persuade the child to choose "something better" neither cures the cause nor encourages an improvement in standards of choice.

It is very difficult at any time to discover exactly what a child is taking from a book. It may, in fact, be something very different from anything the adult mind supposes the book does or does not offer. Let me try to suggest an example by instancing books like those about Nancy Drew and the Hardy Boys and the stories of the prolific English author, Enid Blyton, all of it work which is criticized for its triviality, quantity (the argument goes that children need never and might never read anything else), linguistically impoverished style, anemia of characterization, and clichéd, stereotyped ideas and plots. I suspect that this very absence of quality is what makes such stuff attractive to children, not just because it is easy to read, undemanding, untaxing, but because the simplistic plots and characters leave children free to embroider and enrich the stories *in their own way* as they read. The author provides an outline; the young reader uses the outline on which to graft his own refinements.

On the other hand the more resourceful the literature, the less it can be read in this way. You cannot, for example, "play with" the novels of Virginia Hamilton or those of the Cleavers, or — the best English example of this other extreme — of William Mayne. You have to give yourself up to these writers, allowing them to guide you through their alternative world in their own ways. In terms of literary criticism, Hamilton, the Cleavers, and Mayne will come out best over the Hardys, Nancy Drew, and Blyton's various mystery and adventure stories. Only in one major respect will the rubbish writers come out best. They are skilled at writing "what-happens-next?" action-full plots that keep you turning their pages.

But my whole point is that in reading rubbish children are not — and are not wanting to be — engaged in reading for literary satisfactions. Anyone who has taught drama knows that children love being given an outline story to set them off on improvised drama-play. Having got started they begin to shape the original outline to their own ends, often making it something quite different and completely their own. I believe they sometimes read in this way, using books for interior improvisation. I am not suggesting children do this every time they read a book. But they do read like this often and, I think, need to just as much as they need outward play.

There is an interesting experiment for testing this idea. Think of a book which gave you great pleasure as a child but which you have not read since. Remark every detail that you can remember. Then find a copy and reread it. The surprising thing to me when I tried this experiment was that many of the details I could remember were not in fact in the text at all. What is more, the text itself — with some notable exceptions — was unbelievably "thin." The nonexistent details were, I presume, my own inventions, and the remembered fullness of the text a creation of my own reworking of the original "outline" or "script." The notable exceptions I mention are, of course, the great books, and the reverse is true about these. I remember less about them than, on every rereading, I discover they possess. The great books always have something new to reveal. *The Wind in the Willows* is, for me, in this category, for example, while *Mr Bumbletoes of Bimbleton*, the book I used for my experiment (now regrettably out of print, and, for most people no doubt, out of mind), is in the category of "interior play scripts."

What we are discussing then is two ways of reading: the literary and the nonliterary referred to in Chapter one. And it is pointless to argue whether one is *the* essential way of reading and the other something to be suppressed, if it is true, as I suggest, that children need both. They are not in opposition, as people think when they worry about rubbish. All that has to be said is that once children start reading they will find their own non-literary material without wanting help from teachers; whereas to become literary readers they do need help.

One last thought. How often have we actually read what we condemn as rubbish? And how sure are we that it is rubbish after all? Peter Dickinson in an article "A Defense of Rubbish" expressed what I have in mind:

> The adult eye is not necessarily a perfect instrument for discerning certain sorts of values. Elements — and this particularly applies to science fiction . . . — may be so obviously rubbishy that one is tempted to dismiss the whole product as rubbish. But among those elements there may be something new and strange to which one is not accustomed, and which one may not be able to assimilate oneself, as an adult, because of the sheer awfulness of the rest of the stuff; but the innocence — I suppose there is no other word — of the child's eye can take or leave in a way that I feel an adult cannot, and can acquire valuable stimuli from things which appear otherwise overgrown with a mass of weeds and nonsense.*

Worrying about the rubbish is a fruitless business. The time and energy is much better spent bringing children into touch with the whole body of their rich literary inheritance.

*Peter Dickinson, "A Defense of Rubbish," *Children's literature in education*, No. 3 (Nov. 1970) p. 7.

X

Book Buying: Book Owning

A relentless logic has turned many teachers into mini-book-sellers. Everything they know from theory and practice about the growth of literacy beyond a merely adequate minimum ability to obtain the simplest information and instruction points to the importance of book ownership as both a reflection of, and a formative influence on, a family's attitude to reading. What are called "advantaged" homes, by which we mean those that offer their children the benefits every child should have, possess their own small libraries. But most children are, in this respect at least, disadvantaged: their homes possess few books, if any. At Christmas and on birthdays there might be some among the other presents, and if one of the family has a passionate interest in a hobby or pastime, a book, usually of the information kind, is found to satisfy his curiosity. But the idea of buying books as you buy clothes or groceries is an alien one.

Most parents are not like Prospero, who valued books above his dukedom, nor do they think as did Sydney Smith "no furniture so charming as books." They may genuinely want a better education for their children, and may often understand that reading lies at the heart of the matter. But because book ownership is something removed from their normal pattern of life, a pattern they grew up accepting, it is difficult to explain how strong is the connection between owning books and appreciating them fully, between buying books and reading them. After all, they argue, there are the so-called "free" public libraries: self-service stores where you can go and get books without paying for them. So why pay good money just to own the things and have them collecting dust around the house? Against that kind of thinking it is pointless to quote research figures and surveys and reports that provide evidence time and again of the importance of book ownership in the acquisition of the "better education" everybody wants for their children.

So teachers find themselves laboring against the grain. Educational theory is based upon the assumption that the home environment complements the school; that it provides a background fertile for the child's educational development. Yet it is patently clear, so far as reading and books are concerned, that most homes play no such role. It is a theory built upon an assumption about a certain minority — those brought up in literate surroundings — and transferred as though it still held true to a majority living under quite different circumstances.

What do teachers do? Do they tackle the problem? Do they try by one method or another to awaken parents and children to the importance of owning books? Is such activity a proper part of their task; does it lie within the bounds of their responsibility? Ought they to spend time in this way? And how do they do it anyway?

Once an interplay between true literacy and book ownership has been convincingly established (and no one who thinks about it for two minutes and looks at the ever more numerous reports on reading and literacy can doubt that it has been) these questions must be answered. We find ourselves in a dilemma. Teachers are primarily charged with the education of children, but they are hindered in the discharge of their responsibility by an absence in the majority of homes of a cultural precondition that enables them to teach properly — and teach not only literature but everything else which depends on the printed word. They know what the precondition is; and they know that one aspect of it is the attitude to books in the home. Either they can labor on in the hope that someone else will do something about it, or they can do something about it themselves. And if they choose to do something themselves, they must readjust their thinking about educational methods and their responsibilities. They must be convinced that giving time to encourage children to buy books — indeed, giving time actually to sell books — is a directly educational activity. And they must consider that the education of parents lies legitimately within the bounds of their work.

Teachers who have seen that they must tackle the problem have on the whole managed to find ways of encouraging book buying. The task would have been easier (though probably less necessary, too) had bookshops been commonplace round the country, or indeed if booksellers had been as vigorous in their business as grocers and insurance agents in theirs. Good bookshops are few and far between; and the kind to be found in most towns, hybrid affairs dealing in newspapers, magazines, stationery, trinkets and a motley collection of paperbacks in revolving wire racks is about as educationally healthy as a river rich in industrial effluent is physically salubrious.

Opinions differ as to the best method for teachers to use. There are several, and which one to try depends somewhat on local circumstances, the available bookshops, the organizing teacher's aims, and the extent to which the school authorities, in particular principals, are prepared to go.

THE SCHOOL BOOKSHOP

This is the most complete and permanent arrangement. An agreement is made with a bookseller by which the school becomes an agency, a branch in effect, of his store. The bookseller is responsible for supplying the books, dealing with publishers, suppliers, and all financial matters. The school, through the organizing teacher, looks after the day-to-day management of the "shop"; fixing opening times, manning the counter, looking after the stock, informing the bookseller about orders and when fresh stock is needed, and accounting the money and sales. To make this system work well there must be close cooperation between school and bookseller; and the bookseller will, of course, look for some profit from his involvement, though it is likely to be very small. The school can expect very little financial return but will know that there is expert help behind the venture and that it is released from a great deal of clerical work and financial risk.

Some schools run the very simplest of shops, no more than a portable cupboard containing a couple of hundred paperbacks which are put on sale once a week. Other schools elaborate on this. A table is set up in a classroom, books are laid out on it by pupil "shop assistants" supervised by a rota of teachers, and regular opening hours are laid down and adhered to. Stock is stored in a cupboard when the shop is closed and some care is taken to advertise and promote sales. Nearer the ideal, there are schools which have managed to convert a room into a permanent, self-contained shop, an enterprise that needs enthusiasm from staff, pupils, and parents. The ideal itself, attained by a few schools, is a specially designed bookshop built as part of the premises, properly sited, equipped with shelves, display space, counter, and all the correct fittings.

However rudimentary or advanced the system, and no matter what the age of the children involved, certain matters should be considered before setting out on the venture.

1.   More than one member of staff ought to be directly in charge of the day-to-day organization. It is too much for one person to carry the load unaided. Furthermore, considerable sums of money may be involved and must be properly handled. Absence from school of the only organizer means that errors creep in very quickly, or that the shop has to be closed. And should the organizer leave altogether, the shop is likely to close for good. The whole value of a school owning its own bookshop lies in its permanence as a school institution and the continuing use of it by the children.

2.   The responsibilities to be shared between the commercial bookseller, if there is one involved, and the school should be sorted out at the beginning. Whatever is agreed to, one thing should always be understood: that selection of stock is, in the end, the school's province. A good bookseller will know what sells well; but the school must, for its own protection, have the final say should disagreement arise in this area.

3.   Teachers should not be the only ones to make decisions about stock on the school's behalf, however. Children have ideas to contribute and they should be listened to. They ought also to help organize and run the business, just as pupils help in the library. This may be arranged through a bookshop committee. Each class can also send in monthly suggestion lists after dis-

cussions in lesson time. Preparation of publicity posters, publication of the bookshop news-sheet: there are all kinds of ways that lead to participation by children.

4. For the most part, the stock will be made up of paperbacks: priced within the range of schoolchildren's pockets, they are also the format young people find most attractive. Experience will tell how many and which hardbacks to put on sale.

5. Even with the closest supervision some books will be lost through theft, a fact of life one must recognize and cope with. Temptation and opportunity should be kept to a minimum without at the same time imposing a restrictive and suspicious atmosphere on the proceedings. A good deal can be achieved in the right direction by careful planning during selling times. A cash desk should be placed by each exit. Each display point should be supervised by an assistant, either a pupil bookseller or a member of staff. Proper security during closed times — locks on stock cupboards and a limit to the number of keyholders — is an obvious precaution.

6. Good publicity helps a school shop as it does any other.
   i.   Opening times need plenty of announcement.
   ii. Posters, made perhaps by pupils as well as by staff or bought from publishers and other sources, draw attention to the shop and to specific books.
   iii. Display boards show book jackets, author-photographs, what the trade calls TV and film "tie-in" material to promote topical books.
   iv. Special occasions organized by the shop (visits by authors, book fairs, and the like) help keep book buying in the children's minds.
   v.   Savings schemes are set up to help children save from their allowances for books they want to buy.
   vi. The shop may have its own "Book tokens" — gift vouchers that people can buy and which are redeemable only at the school bookshop.
   vii. The shop should be in evidence and open at every major school function, like open house days, plays, sports events.

7. In many teachers' experience a school bookshop begins with a rush of business which tails off after a few weeks. To some extent, this is something anyone might expect to happen, and it is not a sign of failure. On the other hand, the object is to sell books regularly to as many children as possible, and settling down with a steady clientele of kids who are readers anyway should satisfy no one. So the initial interest must be consolidated as quickly as possible. The first weeks are vital, and after that the shop must be constantly on the lookout for ways of stimulating further interest and re-awakening those who lapse. Gimmicky events are not very useful: they entertain for a while but do not put book buying and reading at the center of attention. Less gaudy techniques are usually in the end more successful. "Focus weeks," for instance, provide a boost in special directions, as when the shop puts on a show of sports books arranged perhaps in conjunction with a big match or sports event in the school. The chances are that children who are interested in the sport will come to the shop to see the show whether they are readers or not, and so make contact when otherwise they might not have done. What matters above all is the feeling of energy, of liveliness, of things going on: this is what will attract customers and keep them.

8. Obviously the work of the bookshop must be tied in to the work of the school library so that they reinforce and help each other. There are psychological advantages, though, in running them as separate enterprises, rather than the bookshop being part of the library's service to the school. Some children are prepared to patronize the shop, and use it in quite a different way, when they find the library (however well run) stuffy or off-putting. The shop should always be "theirs" in the way that the library cannot be because it must serve all the academic and educational interests of the school, both staff and pupils. The shop — outwardly and in atmosphere at least — is about the children's own, leisure interests (even though it will stock books the children need to buy for study purposes).

Unless teachers are prepared to give thought to topics of this sort, and unless they are prepared to cope enthusiastically with an administrative responsibility that demands a lot of time, they had best not begin a bookshop at all. There are other methods of helping children become book buyers that are less demanding and easier to operate.

BOOK FAIRS

These are bumper book sales arranged to suit the school's convenience, though three a year are the most that can be properly managed and many schools who organize them find one or two enough (often held in November in U.S.A., in October in U.K. during Children's Book Week or in April during Library Week in U.S.A.). Children, staff, parents, people from the neighborhood are all invited to help, visit, join in the peripheral "sideshows," and buy books. Once again careful planning pays dividends, and plenty of time and helpers are needed.

There is now a wealth of experience gained by teachers who have organized fairs, and it is useful to talk to some who have taken part in them. A small fair lasting only a day, such as might be held in a kindergarten or small elementary school can get by with a couple of members of staff and a parent as the organizing committee. Those held in big schools that last several days and are supported by exhibitions and linked activities require a commensurately larger collection of staff and children. In any case it is best to split up the work among all those involved, having an adult in charge of each "department."

These are some of the main items to be considered:

1. *Time*   A fair cannot be put on at a few days' notice. A decision has to be made at least three months before, allowing time to collect helpers, arrange for the supply of books, prepare publicity, make displays and exhibits, and obtain speakers. Book supply, for instance, can take six weeks or more, regardless of quantity.

The date for the fair often suggests itself, and, of course, must be fitted into the school program so that it does not clash with any rival local or national event. November or early December is a good time because people have presents in mind for Christmas; a couple of weeks before spring and summer vacations helps promote holiday reading. National, local and school celebrations like Children's Book Week, International Children's Book Day, centenaries of famous authors, and the like provide focal dates.

The duration of the fair depends on many factors. A small country school can do in an afternoon and evening the same job for its community as a big city high school will take at least two days and more likely a whole week to achieve. The aim is to provide enough time for every child and all parents to browse and buy. This means that during the day groups of children look round the fair, and buy if they wish, or make lists of books they would like to have so that they can tell their parents what to buy for them. In the evenings and perhaps all day on a Saturday, the fair is open for visits from parents and friends as well as pupils. It is important that no one should be hustled through too quickly.

2. *Where?* There should be plenty of space to lay out all the books attractively and for people to move about without feeling too crowded. School halls make obvious sites; and large school libraries (if carefully prepared) are also suitable. If necessary more than one room can be used, but they should be close together, easily accessible and preferably on the ground floor. Large clear notices outside and inside the school should indicate what is being held and where. Car parking facilities will be needed and should be manned during the hours when open to the public. Toilet facilities should be available and well signposted.

3. *Book Supply*   The easiest and most efficient method is to use a bookseller who provides all the books. The firm does not have to be near at hand, but there must be plenty of cooperation and consultation as to selection of stock. Whichever bookseller is approached — and a number may have to be before one is found who is willing to help — it is a point of wisdom to assure oneself of capabilities and the conditions they will impose before any arrangement is made.

A school can, of course, attempt to gather the books without the help of a bookseller, but this is exhausting and can be tricky.

4. *Book Selection* Whatever method of supply is used, it is essential that the school have some control over what is put on sale. But everyone must also realize that a fair is unlikely to be successful, commercially or otherwise, unless a broad selection of books is displayed. Certainly the school and public librarian, class teachers, parents, and children themselves can be consulted and their ideas taken account of, as well as the advice given by book-sellers and suppliers who know which titles will be popular. Most schools favor paperback fairs for the reasons already given about cost and format. Each time a fair is held experience about selection will be gained, as well as about organization as a whole.

5. *Publicity* Very important, and the more the better. Teachers and children should know at least a month beforehand the details of what is going to happen, and after the first announcement there should be a gradual buildup of anticipation by a planned program of information about events and attractions. Publicity directed at parents and the neighborhood should start going out from three weeks before the date.

Posters made by pupils can be got into local stores, banks, offices, libraries, and anywhere else that people will allow. Also, of course, around the school.

Letters to parents announcing the fair and inviting them to visit it, giving dates, times, activities arranged, are best sent through pupils about ten days before.

The local press will often take an interest, printing news "stories" about the fair. Local radio and TV should be approached.

6. *Layout* A decision has to be made about whether the books will be displayed higgledy-piggledy or according to a plan. Some schools favor subject arrangement, others group together everything by publisher, and others sort everything out according to a theme. There seems to be no consensus of opinion about what succeeds best. Whatever the plan, notices should help visitors find their way among the books.

Always set the books out so that they show their fronts rather than their spines; and every copy should be within easy reach without others being knocked about.

Naturally people will handle books before they decide to buy them, which means that no more than a couple of copies of each title should be put out so that reserve stock is prevented from getting grubby. "Assistants," each in charge of a section, will see that their bit is kept tidy and refurbished, while keeping an eye open for thieves.

Usually, tables are used on which to display the stock; decorated cardboard boxes and other objects may be used on the tables to help vary the landscape and provide background. Shelves designed to hold front-facing books are naturally very useful if any are available.

7. *Selling Points*   Restrict these to an efficient minimum — enough to cover exits from the rooms used. There should always be a responsible adult in charge, with a pupil assistant to put the bought books into paper bags and another to record sales by title and author, something that will be found useful not only in checking stock at the end of the fair but also in making decisions about selection for future events.

8. *Side-Shows*   Experience indicates that fairs which include additional attractions besides the "core collection" of books sell more than those which do not. These can be as inventive as one cares to make them, but with one proviso: they should not be so diverting that they are visited for themselves alone. They should attract people into the sale, not from it. The following are some well-tried activities.

Talks by authors, illustrators, publishers. These should be well advertised and fixed for times when the largest audience can be expected. Expenses should always be paid and when possible a fee also. Many authors and special guests are glad to help in this way in the cause of book promotion, particularly when they live locally, but they should still be treated properly in the ways discussed in Chapter eleven, "Star Performers."

Storytelling and reading in a room set apart from the sale-rooms and led by competent people can be either an entertainment designed for all, or a way of solving the baby brother and sister problem, while parents visit the sale. These sessions can be "straight" or can involve video recordings or film-strips.

Film shows. Short films about authors exemplify what I mean by attracting to the sale, rather than detracting from it. Being short, they do not occupy visitors for too long, and being about well-known authors they may attract some people to buy their books.

Models and displays set up in the salesrooms or as special exhibits are both decorative and interesting. They may comprise work done by pupils or hired from outside.

Plays and music performances in short program put on by staff and children at set times are always popular and require less arduous preparation than a full-length public performance. Scenes from books done in polished improvisations, for instance, or puppet plays adapted from stories are just right.

Refreshments prepared and served by parents, staff, and pupils during public opening hours are always welcomed by visitors and are often the only profit-making part of the occasion!

9. *Follow-up* At the end of the sale, the main and least pleasant job is to sort out all remaining stock and check it against sales, as well as to dismantle display stands, exhibits, and publicity notices. When this is over, however, and everyone has had time to think, discussions should be held with helpers in which all details are gone over and suggestions made for improvements in the future. The school as a whole should also be given the chance to voice opinions and ideas, and class teachers should be encouraged to talk with their pupils about books they bought at the sale as a way of consolidating the work.

A book fair is a big occasion and ought to appear so. It should be colorfully presented and exciting to visit. As a means of encouraging the book-buying habit, however, it is useful only if regularly held at least once every school year. Ideally, fairs should lead to the introduction of a shop and should then be booster occasions helping to support children's buying habits.

XI
Star Performers

My friends read my books not because they think I am any great shakes as a writer but simply because they know me. This is the only reason anyone needs for inviting authors in particular, out of all the professional book people, to meet children. Publicists — for good or ill — have learned their lesson: get an author on television to talk about himself and his work, and up go his sales; put him on the lecture circuit so that he meets people who often had never heard of him before and the warehouse stock sheets graph his progress round the country. Profiles in newspapers and magazines, autograph-signing appearances in bookshops — any device at all that reveals the person behind the book does far more for an author's readership than yards of reviews or pages of expensive advertisements.

It is, surely, only natural. Children respond no less than adults (rather more, in fact) to personal contact. Popular authors receive scores, in some cases hundreds, of letters a year from their young readers and every correspondent, I am quite sure, wants a reply. Maybe they are all trying to answer the question a little girl once asked me: "Do real people write books?" Real people do. And sometimes when you meet the "reality" face to face you wonder how its owner ever managed to author anything and find yourself put off his books for life. But it is true nevertheless that by meeting authors (the plural is important) and asking them questions, talking about their books, doing things with them, children are drawn into a permanent involvement with literature. Cold print takes on a human voice; wadges of paper covered with words turn into treasured troves full of interest.

Authors-in-the-flesh bridge the gap between children and

books in a fashion no one else can. Not because they have more skill than teachers or anyone else, but simply because they are authors: the people who created the books themselves. And it is always more interesting as well as enlightening to talk to the person who made the goods than to the person selling them.

Children's writers usually welcome opportunities to meet their audience. A writer's job is seldom glamorous, usually difficult and always lonely. A day away from it now and then, mixing with children, hearing their opinions, trying to answer their questions, can be an invigorating relief. And at worst, if the trip is a flop (it happens!), at least he is glad to get back to work. One should never hesitate to invite authors to visit children. But there are practical problems that need attention.

CHOICE

Choosing who to invite often decides itself. Children and teacher have, for instance, read a book and been especially excited by it. Asking the author to visit is a natural step to take. And it is even more obvious in the case of books set for exam or class study. Some authors, of course, object to their work being subjected to compulsory dissection for exams in the traditional deadly manner. Like Bernard Shaw, they swear to haunt anyone who so mistreats them (Shaw's ghost must be busy these days). Apart from this, some authors' books are very popular as set texts, and so they cannot possibly accept all requests or they would never write again. Discretion is needed, therefore.

Recommendation by people who have seen them performing well with children — and not all have the gift — is another way of coming across authors worth inviting. A study topic in, say, history may suggest others. Then there are authors whose books are demanding: meeting them may well provide the stimulus some children need to read what they have written.

Over a period of time, two or three years, any one group of children should meet a mixture of writers: some whose books they know well and like, some who are new, some who produce information books, some who talk about their work and themselves, some who prefer to do things with the children. As time goes on and the list lengthens, the hope is that children will respond to the infinite variety that books encompass. I am never quite sure what people mean when they speak of things being "relevant"; but this sense of involvement, of living application and belonging is what I mean. And bringing writers of all kinds together with children helps everyone discover that pertinent relationship.

MAKING THE APPROACH

When a private address is not known, authors are most easily reached through their publishers, although letters should be sent in plenty of time for a busy mail room to take care of forwarding them. Better yet would be to inquire of the publicity, or Library Services Department, as most U.S.A. publishing houses now title their promotion departments, if that author is available for speaking engagements. The library services person will then give you the author's address, if he does accept engagements, or, often, make a preliminary inquiry for you. The library services people like to know if an author is requested as a speaker, and they also may suggest authors and illustrators near at hand who are new to the region, or perhaps not known to the teachers and the school.

An initial letter of invitation should include a stamped, self-addressed envelope and, to avoid unnecessary further correspondence, should provide at least the following details:

1. Your own and/or the school's name, address, telephone number.
2. An outline of the reason why you are inviting the author to visit, what you would like him to do, the age and numbers of the children likely to be involved.
3. A selection of dates suitable to yourself, leaving the author free to choose the one most convenient.
4. The fee and expenses you can offer.
5. The accommodation you can arrange should the visit require an overnight stay. (It is not always the case that visitors like to be houseguests of a family; they may prefer a hotel and should be given the option.)
6. The geographical position of the meeting place and its ease

of access from major roads, railway stations or airports. If transport from a railway station or airport is needed, say whether you can provide it.

It is not wise, by the way, to make the first approach by telephone for this puts the author on the spot and he may refuse simply in self-defense — and especially if you happen to butt in when he is struggling with an obstinate chapter in a new book.

Given this kind of information a considered reply is possible and, because the invitation has been made in a business-like and considerate manner, the answer is more likely to be favorable.

Once the invitation has been accepted certain courtesies ought always to be extended:

1.   Because it is usually necessary to make the first approach well before the event, always confirm the arrangement nearer the date. In the same letter give final details about the visit, and when wise to do so, provide a map of the vicinity of the meeting place.

2.   Make sure that someone is responsible for greeting the visitor on arrival, seeing to his needs, and generally making him comfortable.

3.   If the visitor is an author, illustrator, or publisher, some of his work should be on show.

4.   Be sure any mechanical equipment required (tape machines, film projectors, etc.) does actually work, can be replaced at a moment's notice if it breaks down, and is handled by a competent operator. If an artist requests an easel, make sure it is a sturdy one. Also find out if the artist will need large paper panels or huge pads of newsprint to draw on.

5.   If there must be formal introductions and votes of thanks, at least see that what is said about the visitor is correct, that there are no lengthy public speeches that pre-empt the visitor's reason for being there at all, and that matters are kept as unembarrassing as possible.

6.   Find out whether the visitor prefers to have the children on their own, or won't mind members of staff sitting in.

7.   Make sure everyone — those involved and those who are

not — is aware of timetable and room changes and any other administrative abnormalities; and as far as possible prevent any untoward interruptions. (I shall not quickly forget being halted in full flight during a visit to a college to speak to student teachers by the explosive entrance of a lecturer who, without pause for reflection or apology, set about an unfortunate student for not being at a tutorial. Apart from the fact that the lecturer was at fault for not attending to well-announced changes in program, the incident did make one wonder about the way teachers are trained as well as about the nature of some of the people who teach teachers.)

8.   When the visit is over send a letter of thanks: the gesture need not be merely an empty convention.

One would think it hardly necessary to give advice of this sort but harsh experience says otherwise. Anybody who has done a lot of talking in schools and colleges, at meetings in libraries and to professional as well as voluntary associations, has a fund of stories, hilarious in retrospect but irritating at the time, about the extraordinary treatment suffered at the hands of organizers. And there does seem to be a very close relationship between the size of the fee offered and the amount of care and thought taken. You learn to expect the worst when you are working for nothing.

MAKING THE MOST OF A VISIT

The "star performer's" appearance ought to be the only high point; the visitor provides a focus and incentive. In preparation, it is fairly obvious that the children should be told about the coming visit well in advance and be made aware of the author and his work. Displays attract attention, and can include a photograph of the visitor and biographical details as well as any publicity material that might be available from publishers. All this is basic.

What is more important perhaps is the effect that a prospective visit will have on the children's work activities. It will act as a stimulus, providing them with purpose and energy outside the usual run-of-the-mill work. A program consisting of readings, improvised scenes, and scripted extracts from the author's work, or based on it, is the kind of major project I have in mind. Or adaptations might be made by children and recorded on tape. These would be performed shortly before the author's visit, or, of course, during it, for the benefit of all the children who will eventually meet him. In this way it is possible to bring together literary reading, script-writing, drama work of different kinds, craft work — illustrations for scenes in the books, models for displays, posters about the visit, decorations for the room where it is to take place — and, of course, plenty of talk as plans are made, and the work discussed and argued about.

All this has tremendous educational value. I remember with great pleasure, for instance, a class of thirteen-year-old pupils putting on a puppet show they had written and performed for me after seeing their school's production of one of my plays. The puppet play was loosely based on the ideas in mine, but only loosely. The puppets were simple creations: cardboard heads painted and stitched onto pieces of cloth which formed the glove. The theater was made of three draped art-room tables. The script was improvised on an outline which, I gathered, was the result of three sessions' hard talking to decide whose ideas out of the many suggested should be used. The production itself lasted half an hour (at least twice as long as it had ever taken in any of the numerous rehearsals!) and was vastly entertaining throughout. Of one thing I am certain: nothing I could have done for or with those children would have been half so valuable as all they did for themselves, with their teacher to fall back on when necessary. My value was as a catalyst, an agent which the teacher could introduce into his everyday work as a way of adding something extra that gave intensity and excitement. And I was happy to be of that little use. Just by being a stranger who was also that odd fish, a writer, I had helped to create a context in which the reading those children had to do in preparing their play, the writing, the concentrated talking, the play rehearsing in recess and after school as well as in lesson time, and the final production itself were no longer school exercises imposed, in their eyes, with little reason and less fun.

What is absolutely certain is that without some preparation

by the teacher, a visitor cannot hope to achieve very much; he is in little better a position than cold fish on a marble slab. There is no strong interest to build on and he has to start by creating it — which brings me to the visit itself. It should not be assumed that this has got to be a semiformal talk, followed by a few half-hearted questions: a kind of General's visit to the barracks. The guest might be better employed seeing small groups — half a dozen or so — for quarter of an hour, when they could chat about anything that crops up. Where there have been elaborate preliminary projects, it may be better to center everything on these. Or the author may prefer to base everything on his work, reading from it and discussing with the children. Whatever is decided upon, it seems to me a mistake not to allow time and opportunity for children to meet the visitor on their own. Too often guests are snatched up on arrival and closeted away from the children before being produced like a rabbit out of a hat for the "official" appearance, which is no sooner over than they are hustled off once again, out of reach of anyone but members of staff or the organizer's chosen associates. No doubt this is done out of consideration for the visitor, and going into a school as a "star performer" is certainly a strain. But it is the value to the children of these occasions that we are looking for, and if one takes on such a job one expects to work hard. It is far better, it seems to me, to pay a visitor well and arrange plenty to do, than to pay badly and be satisfied with a few minutes' talk. Exactly how much time should be spent letting children meet the visitor informally and how this might best be arranged is something to be discussed with the guest before the event.

Finally, out of sight should not mean out of mind. True, a visit may have been so disastrous that it is best forgotten; but this is not usually the case. Most "star performers" leave behind some new interest that ought to be nurtured and strengthened. And this throws up lines of approach. Those children whose appetites were whetted need to be sought out and the books they want made available. (A point that might be anticipated: stocks could be obtained before the visit ready for this moment.) Some lesson time should be given up to discussing the visit, answering questions left unanswered and generally consolidating the experience.

PAYMENT

Some fees paid to visiting speakers are no less than insulting. Based, as they seem to be, on some kind of time-on-the-job calculation, they take into account neither the professional worth nor the practical realities of the work. Frequently, even this pittance is refused to teachers wanting to pay an author for a school visit, because it does not fit in with some spurious bureaucratic regulation. The trouble lies in the rigidity of a single basic fee. A one-hour session by an author in a local school costs him in time and effort far less than a full day spent in a school many miles from home. Anyone can appreciate that the same fee paid for both jobs is neither just nor practicable. But that is what tends to be the rule. Similarly, it is naïve to suppose that the same fee for the same work can be offered to an established literary figure much in demand and an emergent writer whom a teacher has happened upon by accident. There should be flexibility in fees, some room for negotiation between teacher and visitor. And there should also be a far more realistic basic scale.

Throughout this chapter I have spoken of authors making visits. But other people can be as effective. Authors seem to have the most curiosity value, that's all. Publishers have much to offer children, and librarians, booksellers, printers, all have obvious parts to play in widening the appeal of books, and children's knowledge and appreciation of them. Perhaps what they all do more importantly than anything else is to remove the burden from the teachers' shoulders. By seeing and meeting all kinds of people who are involved with the printed word children come to realize that books are more than schoolroom tools, and that they satisfy many needs and provide many pleasures.

PART THREE

Time to Read

XII

Storytelling and Reading Aloud

The oral tradition — stories told aloud — goes right back to the tribe and its communal life. And still today, though there are many people who say they do not enjoy or have no time for literary reading, I have yet to meet anyone who does not like hearing a story. It may be no more than gossip, or jokes, or exchanges of personal anecdote and incident, but it is still story: narrative about people, telling what they did, how they did it, and why. Literature in all its forms grew out of the oral tradition and we cannot emphasize enough how deeply rooted in his early oral experience is everyone's taste for reading. As for introducing books to people during their childhood and adolescence, telling stories and reading aloud are the two most effective methods, each fundamental and essentially important. The reasons are worth isolating briefly before we come to the techniques involved.

To begin with, both methods are appetizers. They stimulate a desire to read for oneself what one has heard told. This is especially crucial at the time when children are learning the mechanics of reading for themselves: the printed material they can cope with at this stage is not only severely limited but too often lacks verbal and imaginative richness, the kind of anemia evident in such unhappy "reading schemes" as "Dick and Jane." Through listening to more satisfying language, from nursery rhymes and tales to folk stories and such modern masterpieces as Sendak's *Where the Wild Things Are*, children are kept in touch with the pleasures that will come as soon as they have achieved a modicum of skill. And later on, when their skills are well developed, the same methods lead them on, widening their reading range, forming their taste, strengthening their capacity to comprehend complex language and to handle and appreciate increasingly uncompromising literature. Without this stimulus many children (and always those who need most help) will tend to settle down at a very low level of proficiency, never reaching out beyond a minimal satisfaction.

As children listen to stories, verse, prose of all kinds, they unconsciously become familiar with the rhythms and structures, the cadences and conventions of the various forms of written language. They are learning how print "sounds," how to "hear" it in their inner ear. Only through listening to words in print being spoken does anyone discover their color, their life, their movement and drama. Most people, children as well as adults, "read too much, too bittily and too quickly; they have no gears in their reading. Many of them make a thin response because they give little body — in terms of tone, manner, emotion, and so on — to their eye-reading; their inner ear is almost dead. They need to hear literature read well, and to practice reading it aloud."* You can read satisfactorily for information without knowing about this, but you cannot appreciate and get full pleasure from literature without it. Storytelling and reading aloud are, therefore, more than good teaching methods by which to introduce books. They are essential, formative factors in everyone's literary education.

But another point must also be considered. The capacity of children to comprehend and enjoy language is frequently ahead of their ability to read. Most obviously this is true of those troubled with reading problems. But it is no less true, only less obvious, of most children, if not all, right up to adulthood (and through adulthood for some people). Listening to books read aloud bridges that gap, making available to children books they are mature enough to appreciate but which they cannot yet read with ease for themselves. Those with reading difficulties, of course, might never acquire enough skill. Hearing books read will then be the only way they can receive the great body of the best literature in their native tongue.

---

*Richard Hoggart, "Teaching Literature to Adults," *About Literature*, vol. 2 of *Speaking to Each Other* (London: Chatto and Windus, 1970) p. 220.

TECHNIQUES COMMON TO BOTH METHODS

In storytelling and reading aloud the principal instrument is the voice. An ugly voice, one that is monotonous or grating, weak in power, incomprehensible or strained, is never likely to receive and retain anyone's attention for long. On the other hand it is not necessary to have a superb actor's voice in order to succeed. Given practice, some careful thought, and perhaps a little training, every voice, except those physically defective, can be made serviceable. Certainly teachers who use their voices as tools of their trade should have no trouble in reaching a competent standard. Considering how necessary vocal control is to the profession, it seems to me very strange that student-teachers receive so little guidance or help in many colleges on this subject.

The first thing to be learnt is how to listen to yourself. Unless you can hear what your voice is doing, you can never be sure it is doing what you want it to do. At first, as in playing the violin or riding a bike, the storyteller or reader is so busy concentrating on the mechanics of the business that he has no time to think about his effect on other people. But after a while, when the mechanics have become second nature, he begins to refine his skill and can be both performer and listener at the same time. In getting this far a tape recorder is a great help and is afterwards a useful aid in rehearsing material to be told or read.

Very quickly, beginners discover the importance of breathing in voice control. Shallow breathing from the chest produces a thin sound that lacks resonance and energy as well as duration. Rather, the air should be brought from the diaphragm, so that the voice gains richness and power, and passages requiring long breaths can be sustained without loss of control. Practice is the only way to come by this facility, and texts like Shakespeare, the Authorized Version of the Bible, Milton, Wordsworth, Shaw and Eliot are the kind to work with because they make the biggest demands on depth of breathing as well as on the reader's skill in organizing the phrasing of the words.

It is little use, though, cultivating a well-controlled voice if what it says is incomprehensible. No one likes that artificial, over-precise articulation acquired by meticulously elocuted people who hang words on the air like so many ice cubes. But lazy delivery, when the words are slurred and poorly shaped, or a thick accent difficult for people from outside the region to understand, are just as bad. It is quite possible to achieve clarity while preserving the personal and local flavor of your speech.

Breath control and clarity of articulation play major roles in projection, the ability to direct vocal sounds to the whole of an audience. This is not difficult to do in a confined space with only a few people present, but as soon as double figures are reached in the audience (as, for example, in a normal-sized class of children) in a room of more than domestic proportions attention must be paid to whether everyone present can hear comfortably. The instinct of unskilled speakers is to add volume, to shout. That is a mistake. They may make themselves heard, but they also coarsen the quality of the sounds they produce, limiting the range and vocal color. Projection is really a matter of energy rather than volume, and the energy comes from the diaphragm, which propels the breath like stones from a catapult so that the words are lobbed from speaker to listeners. This is how actors on stage make themselves heard at the back of the auditorium even when speaking very quietly.

Supporting the technique is an indefinable element: a consciousness of the audience and a desire to reach out to everyone in it, as though to touch them with sound. Projection also has to do with confidence. You have to want to communicate and feel capable of doing so. Self-effacing nervousness causes the epiglottis to tighten, strangling the words in the throat and stiffening the diaphragm so that it is like pulled-out elastic unable to propel anything. The storyteller has in fact to be something of a showman, a performer, before he gets anywhere.

Experience allied with self-criticism develops the art. But preparation — knowing what you are going to do and how you are going to do it — is indispensable to success. In preparing material the first thing to decide is the kind of vocal treatment each piece needs. Folk tales, for example, benefit usually from the conversational manner, the round-the-fireside tale told nevertheless with careful attention to rhythm and phrasing, pace and subtlety of vocal tone. Sendak's *Where the Wild Things Are*, when read aloud to young children as they look at the pictures, needs a firm, quiet voice, until that glorious wordless pictorial passage showing the "wild rumpus," when at least one reader has discovered it is necessary to give a one-man vocal performance of some rumbustious classical music as accompaniment to the viewing of those pages.

Of course, in reading aloud the words are supplied by the text. In storytelling (unless a text has been memorized, which is one way of going about it, as we shall see) the words are the performer's own, and this adds another crucial preparatory problem. Just as delivery must be tuned to suit the kind of material chosen, so must the language used to tell a story. It is, naturally, difficult to demonstrate this in print. But there are written stories which are records of oral storytelling and which show something of the kind of thing I mean. Take, for example, this jocular tale recorded in the Westmorland area of northern England, a tale found in variation in the U.S.A.

> There's some as thinks a farm lad must have a good memory, and there's a tale about it. A farmer had just hired a lad, and he wanted to make sure he had a good memory. Well, in the evening, about nine o'clock, they's been settin' afore t' fire, an' he reckoned he'd try t'lad. "Well," he said tull 'un, "it's time we was going to t' Easy Decree." "What's Easy Decree?" asked t'lad. "Bed's Easy Decree," said t' farmer, "we've lots of odd names for different maks of things here; I ca' my breeches Forty Frappers." "Oh!" says t'lad, "an' what d'ye call the stairs?" "L.K.C."
>
> Then t'lad sees t'cat. "And what d'ye call t' cat?" "That's Grey-Faced Jeffer." "And what d'ye call t'fire?" "Popolorum." "And yer well?" "Resolution." "And yer hay-mew?" "Mount Etna, that's as good a name as I can come by. And now we'll away to this Easy Decree, but think on ye say them words ower to yoursel' till you're perfectly sure on 'em."
>
> Well, next morning, t'lad was up early to put t'fire on. He warn't just looking, and t'fire spread to t'cat's tail, that was just settin' by, and so t'cat felt its tail swinged, and ran out of t'kitchen, towards t'barn. And t'lad, as soon as he saw what was happening, up and shouted: "Now, *Maister, Maister,* come

rise from thy *Easy Decree*, put on thy *Forty Frappers*, and come down *L.K.C.* for the *Grey-Faced Jeffer* has gitten *Popolorum* to his tail, and he's off to *Mount Etna*, without *Resolution*, and all will be burned." "Aye," says t'farmer, "thou's aw reet, lad. Thou's gitten a good memory."*

Collected in 1907 from an oral source, this story depends for its charm and attraction on the colloquial flavour, its dialect, and would lose a lot by being formalized and standardized. A reader who cannot inflect the words as they ought to be should not attempt to perform the piece.

Contrast this with the adaptation of "Yallery Brown" by Alan Garner (he calls the story "the most powerful of all English fairy tales" and one is inclined to agree). Garner retains the folk quality, avoiding "the obscurities of dialect without losing the vivid language." He thereby creates a version many tellers can manage who have no command of the original Lincolnshire. Here is a snatch of Garner's version:

> I was in a fine rage, and should liked to have kicked him, but it was no good, there wasn't enough of him to get my boot against.
>
> But I said to once: "Look here, master, I'll thank you to leave me alone after this, do you hear? I want none of your help, and I'll have nowt more to do with you — see now."
>
> The horrid thing brak out with a screeching laugh, and pointed his brown finger at me.
>
> "Ho ho, Tom!" says he. "You've thanked me, my lad, and I told you not, I told you not!"
>
> "I don't want your help, I tell you!" I yelled at him. "I only want never to see you again, and to have nowt more to do with you. You can go!"
>
> The thing only laughed and screeched and mocked, as long as I went on swearing . . .†

This is brilliant editorial work: it leaves the original qualities untouched, and provides a perfect example of how the story-

---

*Katherine N. Briggs, ed., A *Dictionary of British Folk-Tales*, Pt. A Vol. 2 (London: Routledge and Kegan Paul, 4 vols. 1970-71) p. 66.
†Alan Garner, ed., "Yallery Brown," *The Hamish Hamilton Book of Goblins* (London: Hamish Hamilton, 1969) p. 49.

teller should handle folk material in preparing it for himself. The whole question of the language used in folk stories and the qualities to look for is studied at length by Elizabeth Cook in *The Ordinary and the Fabulous*, a book of inexhaustible value to teachers and all those engaged in storytelling and reading aloud.

I hope I have said enough here to stress the importance of linguistic style and to indicate that for the beginner an urgent task is that he discover the styles most natural to him. Once he has a few pieces at his command, widening his collection is an easier task: he can experiment without anxiety because at each trial the new material can be supported by the old so that his confidence is not undermined if it fails. What ought certainly to be avoided is reliance on the same stock of material, the same stock linguistically or in theme and content. One must be ever open to fresh ideas, new possibilities, always on the look-out for suitable additions to the repertoire.

For a storyteller preparation is like rehearsal for an orchestra. The score is explored for its shape, its structure. There will be passages that need emphasis, and some that need a slow pace, others that need a quickened tempo, and so on. Central to this process is the pause. In the age of Harold Pinter, Samuel Beckett, and Peter Brook we ought all to have learnt the part pause plays in the drama of spoken language. Like sounds, pauses have different lengths, different intensities, can be emphasized or ignored. They frame words, form them into significant phrases, can even alter meaning, and infuse emotion. It is when speakers have no feeling for pause that their speech seems to burble on without any arresting quality. The club bore is a burbler: he has not learnt the eloquence of silence.

Basically, pauses are necessary to meaning. Look at these lines from Act Two, Scene Two of *Macbeth*:

> No; this my hand will rather
> The multitudinous seas incarnadine,
> Making the green one red.

The usual interpretation given is to pause after "No," then again after "incarnadine," and then in the last line to touch lightly on "the" and put an equal emphasis on "green one red."

The first two pauses are straightforward enough; change them or omit them and the meaning becomes confused, or at least difficult to follow. But the last line is troublesome. Some actors, in order to try and help the meaning, pause slightly after "green one," and this is unobjectionable. Michael Hordern, however, in a performance some years back, chose to pause after "green," giving the phrase as:

Making the green . . . one red.

The effect was unusual, but it was somehow also a shade comic, which was not at all the intention.

Meaning aside, pauses are used to mold dramatic shape. This means that several interpretations of a passage might have to be tried both in rehearsal and in performance before a definitive version is found which retains the integrity of the text and also suits the reader. For storytelling and reading aloud are performance arts. They involve a script (even when the words are improvised on the spot), an interpreter (the teller or reader), and an audience, and as in all performances, the audience plays a part in molding the finished work.

Most authorities rightly warn us, however, that telling and reading are not the same as acting. A storyteller is "spinning a yarn," "weaving a tale" with words as his material — the old images suggest the anecdotal, conversational quality that must be striven for. An actor, on the other hand, works through movement quite as much as through words, and frequently has to suggest a character different from himself. The storyteller relies on his own personality: he tells the tale, does not assume in himself the characters in the tale. This is why actors often are poor readers: they want to "play" not "tell."

Of course, it is dangerous to generalize. I am not suggesting that there is but one way to read and tell stories — that characters should never have their own voices and that one should always just "talk" the words. I have indeed emphasized that each piece will require its own style. But they must be styles that fit the performer. Dylan Thomas is an interesting example from this point of view. His natural vocal manner was declamatory and sonorous. He pronounced his poetry (as Hopkins also asked that his should be said) and his marvelous tumbling prose like an inspired orator, which he was. But he could adjust that full-bodied, hall-filling, resonant instrument to fit the demands of a radio microphone without losing a note of the fullness, and that ability made his one of the most compelling radio voices I have ever heard. Thomas was a great verbal performer, but he was never an actor; what you got was Dylan Thomas, *his* language and *his* personality. With timing precise and neat, phrasing skilled and controlled, he designed everything for dramatic effect, and even in his last days when he puffed audibly his breathing still supported his voice and gave it energy. A master of the art, it is death to imitate him, as it is always dangerous to imitate other people. One can learn from the techniques of the great performers and so improve one's own work, but imitation becomes first parody and at last a performance empty of the one thing that matters: a living, voice-carried personality that is one's own.

STORYTELLING

The most commonplace, direct source of storytelling material is personal incident, the kind of thing that in ordinary conversation might be introduced with a phrase like, "You'll never guess what's just happened to me. . . ." Every teacher, I suppose, has his own collection of favorite yarns based on this autobiographical starting point. The usefulness of such an approach is obvious: it very quickly establishes the right tone in the relationship between teacher-storyteller and children-audience. And because the teller is sharing something of himself, the children in their turn respond by wanting to share something of themselves in the same way. This is itself important for they are thus engaged in using language creatively, a preparatory experience that helps them to reach an understanding of what literature is all about.

This is, however, only a starting point, a kind of literary gossip. One also needs a large collection of stories, which will be drawn mostly from printed sources even though one tells them "spontaneously" each time, using no script. There are different ways of handling these.

One method is to learn the story by heart as an actor learns his lines. Some stories, Beatrix Potter's for example, are so written that the words used and their order are essential to the tale. And some stories are so well known, or become so well known to children because they enjoy hearing them again and again, that a cry of protest goes up if the words are changed at all. Material of this nature must be committed to memory — or, at least, the essentially unalterable parts must be — otherwise it is best to read aloud rather than storytell. The method has one big disadvantage: rote-learned material may go stale after a few performances, just as a play may go stale for actors. It is often better therefore to begin by reading a story, either to oneself or to children until the ingredients are familiar — the narrative shape, the plot, the characters, the details of time, place, motive, atmosphere, theme, moments of climax and suspense — and then to tell the story on future occasions in one's own words. The performance is kept fresh each time because the teller is under a tension: he has to find the language in which to clothe the body of the work.

The great storyteller, Frances Clarke Sayers, having advised the beginner to "steep himself in folklore until the elemental themes, the folk wisdom, the simplicity of characterization, the universality of their attitudes, are part of himself," explains how best to get command of a tale:

> After you have chosen a story you long to tell, read it over and over and then analyse it. What in it has appealed to you? The humor?, The ingenuity of the plot? What is its mood? And when you have isolated mood and appeal, consciously, this too will color the telling of the story.
>
> Where is the climax? Make a note of it in your mind, so that you can indicate to the children by pause, by quickening of the pace, the peak of the tale. Then read it again, and over and over. Then see if you can list, or call over in your mind, the order of the events of the story, the hinges of action, in their correct sequence. With these fully in mind, read the tale again, this time for turns of phrase you may want to remember. When these have been incorporated into your story, tell it to yourself, silently, just before you go to sleep at night, or while riding a

bus or subway. After all this, you will find that the story is yours forever. For though you may forget it, after years of neglect, one reading of it will restore it to you, once you have mastered it thoroughly.

Do not memorize a story, unless it is a story by Kipling, Sandburg, or Walter de la Mare, for the great stylists must be memorized, especially when they use language in ways of their own. Half the joy of the *Just So Stories* would be lost if they were told in any language other than that in which Kipling wrote them. Even when a story is memorized, it is well to have gained control of it in the manner which has been here indicated.*

The best material to use in this approach is that great corpus of traditional folk and fairy tale, myth, legend, and stories from Biblical and historical sources. These have particular appeal to children and are especially suited to being told for reasons which Elizabeth Cook has already summed up better than I can in some comments she makes about fairy tales becoming the peculiar property of the nursery only by historical accident:

> Nevertheless the accidents that gave these stories to children were happy ones. Children under eleven are eager to know what happens next, and impatient with anything that stops them from getting on with the story. They want to listen to conversations only if direct speech is the quickest and clearest method of showing what was transacted between two people as a necessary preliminary to what these two people proceeded to do. At about nine or ten they are beginning to be interested in character, but in a very straightforward and moral way: they see people as marked by one particular attribute, cleverness, or kindness, or strictness, or being a good shot, and they mind whether things are right or wrong. They are especially sensitive to the heroic virtue of justice, and they are beginning to notice why people are tempted to be unjust. They are not interested in the long processes of inner debate by which people make difficult decisions, and become very irritated with grown-ups who insist upon giving them not only the practical answer or information they asked for, but also all the reasons for it. They

*Frances Clarke Sayers, "The Storyteller's Art," *Summoned by Books* (New York: Viking Press, 1965) pp. 104-105.

expect a story to be a good yarn, in which the action is swift and the characters are clearly and simply defined. And legends and fairy tales are just like that. Playground games show that children like catastrophes and exhibitions of speed and power, and a clear differentiation between cowboys, cops and spacemen who are good, and Indians, robbers and space monsters who are bad.

Magic has a particular attraction for eight-to-ten-year-olds, but not because it is pretty or "innocent." They delight, in more senses than the usual one, in seeing how far they can go. If some people are taller than others, how tall could anyone conceivably be? If some people are cleverer than others at making things, could someone alter what things are actually made of? If there are different languages which different people understand, could there be a secret language that affected things and people against their will? Such speculations carried *ad infinitum* are given concrete form in giants, and the enchantments of elves and dwarfs, and the magic of runes and spells.*

One could not better describe criteria for selecting stories for telling and reading to children before adolescence than Elizabeth Cook does here. And she goes on to point out a subsidiary quality in this kind of material which is worth remembering:

Stories that lead to doing things are all the more attractive to children, who are active rather than passive creatures. Myths and fairy tales provide an unusually abundant choice of things to do. Largely because they are archetypal and anonymous (in quality, if not in provenance), they will stand reinterpretation in many forms without losing their character. They can be recreated by children not only in words but in drama, in mime, in dance and in painting. Action in them is not fussy, and lends itself to qualitative expression in the movements of the human body and in the shapes and colors of non-figurative painting.†

In summary: storytelling is in many ways far more demanding as an art than reading aloud; more demanding in linguistic

*Elizabeth Cook, *The Ordinary and the Fabulous*, 2nd ed. (Cambridge University Press, 1975) p. 7.
†Ibid, p. 9.

and technical skills, more demanding in preparation. It is an art of great power and educative value, worth all the effort and time it takes to learn and perfect.

READING ALOUD

If storytelling is more demanding on the performer, reading aloud is more demanding on the listener. To begin with, it is a less conversational art, less of a direct communication between teller and listener: there is a physical object, the book-source, in between. But of greater importance than this is the fact that written words are frequently more compacted in meaning, more sophisticated in construction than language used in the spontaneous form of storytelling. So the listener requires more time to receive the meaning, to take in what is happening. He is helped in this if he can see the reader clearly, is close enough to watch the facial expressions which hint at the drama of the text and to feel the personality of the performer.

Younger children, before and after the time they learn to read, like to look at the book as well as at the reader while they listen. Older children feel that compulsion less forcefully. But there are times when it is right that they should have copies of the text in which they can follow the reading if they wish. This is obviously so if we are reading a text in which the language is very much more difficult than the children can yet read for themselves. Seeing the words helps them understand what they are hearing and links sound and sight of new words so that their vocabulary is stretched by a look-hear as well as a look-say method.

There are also times when we want children to attend more closely to a piece of writing than they can by hearing only. Having read a story or poem through once we may want to re-read it, pausing here and there to dwell on a passage, to savor it and talk about it. Unless everyone involved can refer back to the text this cannot be done with complete success. Usually it means the teacher is the only person who says anything. One might almost formulate a principle that the deeper we want to engage the listener in a conscious recognition of many different aspects

and qualities of literature the more necessary it becomes for him
to follow the reading in a text.

If we want to lead children gradually to an awareness of the
qualities in literature, this is how we can do it best: by reading
to them from rich texts and providing opportunities afterwards
for response tested against the written words. This is not a matter
of cold analysis, against which I warned earlier, but rather of
finding patterns: patterns of plot and character and words. As
Elizabeth Cook remarks, children "are often fascinated by con-
sistency for its own sake, liking patterns because they are patterns." And let me stress yet again that I do not mean we should
be constantly stopping in midstream during a reading to ask
questions and provoke discussion. Patterns can only be discovered when we see things as a whole.

These are some of the ways we can handle reading performances:

1.   A whole short story read at a sitting. Nothing at all might be
said afterwards, or discussion may occur spontaneously immediately the reading is over or in a later lesson. After the discussion
everyone may like to hear the story again the better to appreciate
it in the light of what has been said.

2.   A "program" of short stories, poems, prose passages might
be put together and read as a spoken anthology. Between each
piece there should be a brief interlude or linking passage, and
discussion may flow during these interludes or after the program
is over. An example of children using this idea is given on page
155.

3.   One part of a novel or long text may be read in order to whet
the listeners' appetites for reading the book themselves. The
part chosen should have a unity of its own, a wholeness that
offers a complete experience without at the same time giving
away everything.

4.   Serializations that can be contained within a few sessions,
one following another in quick succession, say, all in one week.

5.   Serializations spread over five or six weeks, a little being read
each day. This is a traditional method — I remember a number of

books being read to me like this when I was a child. For all but
older teenaged pupils, it is unwise to spread serialization over
longer than six weeks, and even this is too long for up-to-nine-
year-olds. The time span is determined by the audience's ability
to keep in mind as the reading progresses all the major elements
(details which have plot significance, for instance, and the relationships between characters); once these details become confused or vague in the memory interest and enjoyment are soon
lost and boredom sets in. Of course, this has to do not only with
the total length of time the serialization takes but the time that
elapses between readings, a period that should not exceed one
week. Even then each session should begin with a brief recap of
the previous week's reading and "the story so far."

Reading time has another dimension that needs attention:
the duration of each session. Obviously, the younger the child
the less he can take. Infants may be satisfied by a few minutes of
listening. By the age of ten, twenty to thirty minutes should be
about right for all but "backward" children. And by the end of
high school, forty minutes to an hour is bearable, though at
every stage readings should be treated like play or music performances. There should be "acts" or "movements" with brief
intervals between for relaxing the concentration and the body.
Intervals do not have to be filled with talk, either. They can be
simply "breathing spaces." But always, in every aspect of this
kind of teaching, two factors guide us, indicating what to do.
First, the nature of the material being read and second, the
response of the listeners. A difficult book takes more concentrated attention than something much easier, and this will alter
the length of time children can attend to it. Some books provoke
vocal responses — a kind of literary effervescent effect — while
others seem to turn people in on themselves, when they prefer
to say nothing but savor the reading in silence. I have found,
for example, in reading extracts from Scott's diary of his trip to
the South Pole that fourteen-year-olds interrupted all the time to
ask questions and make observations, until the final entries were
reached, when everyone went very quiet, moved deeply by Scott's
words and unwilling to bruise the emotion they felt. On the
whole, the stronger the emotional power of writing the less chil-

dren want to say about it. And this, to my mind, is something to be respected.

If we have selected well and prepared our readings before-hand, we can afford to relax during "performance": we can give ourselves up to the words, enjoying them as much as we hope the children do, and allowing the session to control itself, to follow its own path, because whatever happens there will be a feeling of rightness about it, of mutual sharing and participation and pleasure. Whether we speak or listen, pause or go on, break off sooner than expected or continue longer than normally, these things will sort themselves out according to the way a number of factors interact on each occasion, factors such as the quality of our performance, the kind of text being read, the receptivity and mood of the audience, the whole set and setting of the event.

The best teachers seem to introduce reading aloud and storytelling into their work with spontaneous ease without at the same time losing any of the sense of drama and specialness, and their children settle down to listen with an unfussy expectation of pleasure to come. The whole business has an air of familiarity because it happens every day; yet it has a freshness and excite-ment too, because there is always something new and enjoyable to be shared. But for a teacher to get himself and his pupils this far requires thought and skill and a genuine belief in, as well as wide knowledge of, all literature. "All of this" wrote Frances Clarke Sayers in summary of the storyteller's art that applies as a summary of everything said here, "demands a great investment of time. Yet there is hardly any other investment, hardly any other area of study, that yields so potent a means of making literature live for children."*

CHILDREN AS STORYTELLERS

An old teacher of mine, a cynical little fellow of no great profes-sional ability, used to tell us that teachers were nothing but broken-down actors who liked the sound of their own voices. We would laugh and mutter that in his case the cap fitted. But

---

*Frances Clarke Sayers, "The Storyteller's Art," *Summoned by Books* (New York: The Viking Press, 1965) p. 106.

he had a point. It is very easy to fall into the trap of enjoying the act of telling stories and reading aloud so much that the children never get a chance. Especially when they are happy enough to sit and listen as long as their teacher likes because he does it so well. A balance is important: children have their part to play in telling and reading.

I have already said that on the whole it is not difficult to stimulate children into telling stories. Beginning with personal anecdotes they can soon be led to invent and embroider imaginatively. And they succeed with oral narrative more easily and satisfyingly than with written stories. They are not so inhibited by all the mechanical and technical problems like spelling, sentence structure, the distractingly slow speed of handwriting that frustrates excitement and coherence and the headlong flow of language. Writing is often a chore; telling stories is an uncluttered pleasure. Certainly if children are to write with any real success and understanding it is a necessary part of their apprenticeship that they first feel their way into the art through the experience gained from seeing the effect of their stories on an audience. Even then the business of setting children exercises in story writing — the old fashioned "composition" — is suspect. The activity should have a reality an "exercise in composition" never can. The stories should be for an audience.

I have described in the following article, quoted in full from *The Horn Book Magazine*, one of the best ways I have so far come across of giving the activity a real purpose. It deals with four books written, illustrated, and "published" by children for children. Two of the authors, Scott Bradley and James Banks, were seven years old; one, Julie Harding, was eleven; one book, a collection of short stories, was by a class of twelve-year-old girls.

LETTER FROM ENGLAND:

Having Fun Feeling Famous

What do *The Moon and Three Stars* by Scott Bradley, *The Cosy Owl* by James Banks, *Where Is Mr Biggles?* by Julie Harding, and *Are You Sitting Comfortably?* by Class 1G at

Grange School, Warmley near Bristol, England, have in common?

Answer: They are all stories written, illustrated, made into books, and "published" by children for children. They are just a few examples — they happen to be lying on my desk — of an increasingly practiced and successful school activity. I expect much the same kind of thing is done in American schools, but I thought I would report what is going on in England because the results can be extraordinary in so many ways, not the least of which is the effect on children — the ones who make the books and the ones they are made for — as readers of literature.

Let's take *Where Is Mr Biggles?* as an example of the basic ingredients. This is a picture book, landscape in format, about the size of *Where the Wild Things Are* (Harper). Julie Harding was eleven when she produced it, the last major piece of work she did in elementary school before graduating to our equivalent of your junior high. Her class teacher began it all by putting on an exhibition of about thirty of the best picture books in the school's infant-class library — books for the five-to-seven-year-olds. "Look at these," she said to Julie's class. "Do you remember any of them from when you were infants? What do you think of them now? If you had to buy books for infants, which ones would you purchase?"

Much browsing. Close inspection. Discussion. Argument, even. Partly, this was informal, out-of-class chat; partly, it was group discussion led by the teacher. And it became enthusiastic, a clue the teacher had been watching for before taking the next step. "How would you all like to make a picture book of your own? Make the book you think the infants would enjoy? If you want to, when they're finished we'll take them to the infants and let them look at them. See which they prefer."

Increased enthusiasm. At first this probably sounded like a good lark, a change from ordinary lessons. The work begins. Suddenly, questions: What *is* a picture book anyway? How is it made? What does it contain besides a story in words and pictures? The picture book form is explored; the manufacture of books looked into. Meanwhile, further discussion about the kind of stories that five-to-sevens most enjoy and that would be best for them. And what must the language be like if young children are to be able to read the books for themselves?

Decisions are made. Stories begin to be roughed out, pictures sketched, layouts planned. Various extremes of excitement and despair ensue. Groans, sweating brows, pencils chewed. There is a need for comfort and encouragement from teacher and friends. The trials and traumas of authorship. No lark this, after all! Deadly serious now. Teacher herself is worked off her shoes coping with appeals for help with grammar, style, spelling, critical judgments and, most of all, providing infusions of energy when authorial spirits run low. The teacher as muse.

Time to manufacture the books themselves. Specific demands suddenly are made: The pages must be stitched, not stapled; staples look amateur, not professional. There must be hard covers. (Teacher has to cadge some board from stock — she had not anticipated this item, and she has a hard time justifying the outlay.) Heavens! there must be dust wrappers, too; the best of the books on exhibition apparently have them, and anyway they also make a book look more professional. The desire to get things close to commercially produced books grows stronger and stronger.

Title pages are prepared. There simply have to be printers' and publishers' names. So this classroom outfit becomes Greenmeadow Publishers and the Pen Close Press. And all proper books also have blurbs. The Greenmeadow books will have them, too. Thus, Mr Biggles:

> Joey was moving but he could not find his friend.
> His friend was an elf called Mr Biggles.
> When they reached their new house, Joey looked
> but there was no Mr Biggles.
> Where could he be?

The spreads are "printed" in handwriting as neat as the authors can manage; drawings are done, full-color crayon or felt-tip splendor. The End written at last. (And, in Julie Harding's case, on the very last page all by itself, this: "A Late Dedication. To All the Teachers at Greenmeadow School.") Six weeks have passed. The last session is a kind of publisher's party. Everyone inspects the new list. More discussion; author-like, almost everyone thinks she or he could do it better and wishes she or he could start over again.

Off the thirty-odd books went to the infants. A nervous few days of silence while the authors tried to concentrate on the more mundane tasks of school. Then a summons. The infants sat, solemn as the Supreme Court, and pronounced judgment. They thought this, and they thought that. Examples of likes and dislikes were indicated. And, it transpired, they had decided to announce a winner: a best book. Shades of Library Association awards and medals! *Where Is Mr Biggles?* is declared ace. The entire text is read before the assembly. And afterwards, a last request. Could the infants please keep all the books? They would like to have them in their library so they can read them again. Why? Because these books are better than the ordinary ones — they know the people who wrote them, and that makes them more exciting. A final glow all round; Julie is forgiven for being the best.

Variations on this pattern are many and obvious. But the central values, the ones to ensure, whatever the modifications, seem to me to be these:

1. The child-author must get involved in all the stages of the book's making, from writing and "printing" to hearing criticism before an audience.

2. This means the activity must be "real," not simply an exercise done for teacher or even for classmates.

3. There must be a mixture of educationally basic activity:

    a. Imaginative invention — not just in writing and drawing but in the book-making, too.

    b. The study of suitable literature and of books as objects (in order to decide how to make one's own).

    c. The practicing of writing and drawing, a drill performed in this activity, not for its own sake (it is deadly dull and therefore has minimum permanent effect) but in order to achieve the highest possible quality of work in the finished object.

    d. The practice of manual craft skills: cutting, stitching, using basic tools, measuring, etc. Again, this drill work gains by the reality of its purpose.

    e. The practice of various kinds of talk, such as planning discussions, giving instructions about how to perform specific tasks and operations (child teaching child), etc. But most important of all: critical discussion — about the books explored as "samplers" and about the books being made by the child-authors.

This last aspect of the activity is the one that yields the most valuable gains. By taking apart (quite literally sometimes) a literary book to see how it works, how it was made — both as text and as object — in order to achieve the same things themselves, children make enormous strides as readers. They begin to see that a piece of literature has a shape, a structure; that on the other side of its pages there is a person, the author, who is speaking to the reader personally, communicating many different kinds of messages. They begin to find out about the richness, the density, the multifaceted nature of a "good" book. And they learn this as much by doing it, by making it, as by observing it.

There remains an element in all this activity which I have not said much about so far but which seems to me to be extremely important, from all points of view, for eventual success. The books I'm talking about were made for children two, three, four, or sometimes even more years younger than the child-authors. Why should this be so crucial? Because it is always easier to discuss literature you have outgrown — which belongs to your past — than it is to discuss work which is new to you or is just beyond your capacity as a reader. The new stuff you have not yet had time to absorb and come to terms with. You do not yet know what you think about it. And what strains your capacity as a person and as a reader therefore strains even more your capacity to formulate any comments at all, except a confession of your inadequacy in the face of the book.

All good critical discussion and writing comes from familiarity with a text and from having grown beyond the nerve-end experience of it. Which explains why the activity I'm describing works so well. The child-author approaches it with so much more vigor and confidence because he is dealing with books that speak to the person he once was; and the book to be written is for an audience composed of readers whom the child-author understands because he was one of that audience himself just long enough ago for the memory to be vivid but no longer a threat.

Over the last two or three years I have seen examples of this kind of literary work produced by high school students who have made picture books for infants and by others who have made short novels for pupils a couple of years younger than themselves. I have even seen learning-to-read books made by seven-year-olds for their preschool and play-group juniors. Of them all, *The Cosy Owl* by James Banks is perhaps the most instructive and moving. James, at seven, was a backward reader. His class began making picture books for children in the reception class (five-year-olds). Not to be left out, James began making his, although privately his teacher had doubts that he could manage to do more than draw the pictures. But he persisted and worked extremely hard, apparently with enormous pleasure. Finally, he produced a story all of eight lines long. This he illustrated with great charm: a double-page spread for the story, a title page, and a concluding one-page picture. He stitched his book into an illustrated cover which he laminated with self-adhesive plastic. The result was a volume that looks like a prototype for the I Can Read books James had used as his pattern. More than all this, the experience turned James into a willing reader. Instead of fighting words with a dogged determination, he got to like them. By becoming an author he turned himself into a reader who discovered how to get pleasure from what other authors have to say.

One last anecdote. *Are You Sitting Comfortably?* is an anthology of short stories written by a group of twelve-year-old girls for seven-year-olds. The stories are illustrated, printed on a small printing machine, ring-bound, and have covers made of yellow card. The girls took their stories and read them aloud in a kind of performance (a story-reading play?) to the children in the elementary schools these young authors once attended themselves. What is especially interesting about these girls is that when they were seven, a group of girls from the same high school came and read their stories out of a bound and printed anthology they had made. Apparently, the first thing this present group did when they arrived in high school was to ask their teacher if they could do what had been done for them five years before.

An elementary school I visited the other day had some child-produced books on display. A few of the authors had also written about the experience of making them. One of the authors ended her piece like this: "I liked writing and publishing my own book because it was fun and because it made me feel famous."

Maybe when that young author looks back in a few years' time, she'll realize just how much more she got out of it than a bit of fun and fame. But for now, having fun and feeling famous will do quite well enough. For this crusty author as well as for that young one.*

Oral story-making prepares the way for such writing and bookmaking and can spring off from things that happen in the local community: robberies, the arrival of strangers, the building of a new housing development and the preparatory demolition work, street accidents, big sports events, a strike: any detail that suggests a crisis of one kind or another into which people, with their strengths and weaknesses emphasized, will be drawn. The local newspaper offers plenty of clues, and children themselves contribute others. From this beginning plots can be developed by children either in groups or as a class, characters can be invented or elaborated from real people. What we as teachers should be doing is helping children to bring together the raw material every author needs before he can put flesh and bone onto a basic idea: maps and charts, photographs and settings taken from life, outline facts about characters — their physical appearances, prejudices, tastes, attitudes, beliefs, opinions, idiosyncrasies. As the raw material accumulates, questions are asked. How would this character behave in this situation? What would X do if Y did this, given all the circumstances we know about them?

At this stage it is not the finished story that matters but rather the imaginative exploration of people and the possibilities of action open to them. The effect is twofold. The children's imaginative powers are exercised and developed. And — the important point in this context — their appreciation of the processes and function of literature is deepened. Because they have worked as an author works they are better equipped to see what can be done with words used imaginatively, and will begin to look at what they read with more searching eyes.

This kind of invention — collecting raw material and fitting it into an imaginative structure — is not something that relies on inspiration or talent or an inventive mind. It can be done at any time by any group of children capable of reading and talking about a given theme for half an hour or so at a time. We are

*Aidan Chambers, "Letter from England: Having Fun Feeling Famous," *The Horn Book Magazine*, April 1982, pp. 213-218.

not seeking polished works of art nor brilliant performances. It is the act of creation that matters and from which the benefits of this method flow.

Other methods put to work along side this shift the emphasis from the creative process to telling stories to each other. These stories may depend on narratives invented by the children if they opt for this (but not otherwise) or on sources which provide the stories whole and which the children can tell in their own way, adapting as they wish. I am not thinking only of specially written children's stories, but of a wide range of material. Every locality, for instance, has its body of folklore which children can discover for themselves in preparation for storytelling sessions devoted to it. I was brought up in County Durham in England very near the setting of The Lambton Worme, a version of which appears in Joseph Jacobs's English Fairy Tales. I first heard the story from my grandfather and it has fascinated me ever since. Yet I do not remember any teacher making use of it in my early schooling, something that seems to me now a strange neglect. This local tale could have been used to set me and my classmates off on a search for the other worme stories that litter the area up and down the east coast of Britain. We'd have found The Laidly Worme of Spindleston Heugh, The Pollard Worme, The Helstone Worme, The Linton Worme, and many others. Discovering these tales, looking out printed versions and comparing them with the oral tradition would have introduced us step by step into the rich lode of folklore, and from there we could have been led on to read the adaptations from folklore in the work of writers like Ian Serraillier, Richard Chase, Christie Harris, Ashley Bryan, and many more, and so at last to the core books: the Norse Sagas, The Iliad and The Odyssey, and so on. Storytelling is for children, as it was for the human race, a participatory art from which is born a literary consciousness which by adulthood has grown into a full-bodied appreciation of the work of the great imaginative writers.

CHILDREN AS READERS-ALOUD

Reading aloud needs a great deal of careful handling when children are the performers. If selection of material is important for an adult reader of skill and experience, how much more important it is for children. And if preparation is indispensable to an adult, how can it be otherwise for a child? Yet we go on asking children to read from sight anything we happen to think they ought to be able to manage, regardless of such common sense. We still behave as though we thought that once a child can decipher individual words, we have taught him to read, when, in fact, we have done no such thing. The unit of reading either silently or aloud is not the single word but the phrase, and the unit of complete expression in print is not so much the sentence as the paragraph. There is a lot of work to be done with children after they have learnt to recognize printed words.

By now it should hardly be necessary to condemn the practice of "reading round the class." Nothing is more deadening, tortuous, and degrading to children as readers as well as to the words they are allowed to garble. Yet it is still a method imposed in some schools: the lazy teacher's refuge from hard work, thoughtful planning and organization, and patience. Reading round the class is essentially so wrong because it is a method that mixes up different purposes. If we want children to listen to something read with enjoyment and for the sake of what is read then we cannot at the same time hope to practice their ability to read aloud well. And if we want to give reading practice, we should see that not only do the children understand what is happening but also that as few of them have to endure the others' difficulties as possible. A musician practices his instrument and his music privately, he does not do it during a concert, at which he performs a finished, rehearsed score as perfectly as he can. The same working rules should apply to children and their reading aloud. There are therefore three main kinds of lesson.

1. *Practice*   In these sessions the techniques of reading aloud are taught not for their own sake, but as part of the preparations, the "rehearsals," for a "performance." The texts chosen should be suited to the particular aspect we wish to concentrate on at each time: phrasing, articulation, breathing, dealing with unfamiliar words. It is not necessary to hold such lessons in large groups.

The children may be split up into ones or twos, or small groups of four or five, depending on the nature of the work in hand. Tape recorders can be put to work, individual children using them to listen to themselves and their reading. There can be plenty of instruction and criticism between teacher and taught and among children within their groups. At the outset each time, the children are told clearly what is being asked of them and what is being looked for — what aspect of the work is to be concentrated on. And never is the activity sullied and warped by competition between children to see whether one can read "better" than another. Nor are these training periods held in a purposeless vacuum: they are like the musician's work on scales and fingering and fundamental techniques, the ground-work on which is built the ability to perform for other people's enjoyment. There is always eventually a goal: a time when the art is to be used.

2. *Preparation (or rehearsal)*   These lessons follow on from the above and are concerned with specific texts which are to be read aloud. The actor is preparing his lines, so to speak. Let us suppose that a group of ten-year-olds of mixed ability are preparing a "program" of readings about cats. They have chosen, with the teacher's help, a collection including a few poems, a reading of part of Kipling's *The Cat That Walked by Himself,* and a dramatized reading of the Cheshire Cat passage from *Alice in Wonderland.* All the children involved will work together. Having read through their allotted material silently until they are familiar with it, they begin to read aloud to each other, listening to criticisms and suggestions about how their performance might be improved. The teacher, who may well be dealing with two or three other groups at the same time, will join in from time to time to guide, correct, and help. When the material was being shared out he will have made sure that every member of the group got something that was within his reading capabilities after a certain amount of practice. The Kipling story, as probably the most difficult piece, will be in the hands of the most developed performer. Any children with reading problems will have something very much less demanding but which can at the same time be enjoyed for its own sake — a short poem, perhaps, or a few

words after each piece, linking the one with the next. Part of the group's task will be to dramatize the Cheshire Cat sequence, and to prepare scripts for it, which may end up as a play-reading for three voices:

> NARRATOR: Alice was a little startled by seeing the Cheshire Cat sitting on a bough of a tree a few yards off. The cat only grinned when it saw her.
>
> ALICE: It looks good natured.
>
> NARRATOR: She thought. Still — it had very long claws and a great many teeth, so she felt that it ought to be treated with respect.
>
> ALICE: Cheshire Puss.
>
> NARRATOR: She began, rather timidly, as she did not know whether it would like the name: however, it only grinned a little wider.
>
> ALICE: Come, it's pleased so far.
>
> NARRATOR: Thought Alice, and she said:
>
> ALICE: Would you tell me, please, which way I ought to go from here?
>
> CAT: That depends a good deal on where you want to get to.
>
> ALICE: I don't much care where —

And so on. When the children are working individually instead of in groups they can be put together in pairs to help each other.

3. *The Reading Performance* Everything said about a teacher reading aloud, and about set and setting for the activity, applies here. The primary aim is that whatever is read should be enjoyed. I have suggested the idea of "programs" done by groups of children, but there are other ideas worth using:

(i) "Your story time" — a period set aside for one pupil to read his own selection of prose or verse. These sessions may be only a few minutes long or take up a whole session, depending on the child's age and ability. He will know well in advance when he is to perform and will have selected his material and rehearsed with the aid of his teacher. Children who are upset by an "audience" or who cannot sustain their reading for very long might be helped by recording their performance. This can be done over a number of days, their reading being taped in short passages which can be prepared and then recorded as often as necessary until they manage a satisfactory version. This same technique can, of course, be elaborated upon and used to create items similar to radio programs for playing to other classes or groups. It has the added advantage that the children involved hear their own work, when they tend to be much more self-critical than they are without such an aid.

(ii) Dramatized readings, when a story or poem is prepared on the lines demonstrated, in the Cheshire Cat passage above, are entertaining and also involve children in a number of worthwhile procedures. They must, for example, prepare the script, which necessitates discussion of the text and how properly to interpret it, a basically critical exercise of a valuable kind. Because each child has only one bit to read, he can concentrate on the vocal presentation of that single part without having to worry about all the other different parts as he would have to if he were reading the entire piece. This also means that children of varying abilities can work together, for among the single parts there will usually be some of slight difficulty and short length.

Of course, not all material can be treated like this. The most suitable includes plenty of dialogue, or, at any rate, opportunities for different voices to add something by way of variety and texture as well as enhanced meaning. Undoubtedly this kind of choral adaptation of prose and verse when well prepared and presented is attractive and entertaining to listen to and should form part of the work done by children from seven years old on.

(iii) It is not necessary to hold readings before a whole class. There can be times when the class is divided into groups, each member of each group giving his reading in turn. For preparation the groups have a different composition so that when the readings are finally performed no one has been present at anyone else's rehearsals, and so everyone is hearing the readings for the first time. Alternatively, of course, one class can prepare a program for performance before another class, or before the whole school, or before a class in a neighboring school. This kind of hierarchy of occasions varies the creative tension and keeps the activity fresh and stimulating: there is always an incentive, something to be worked towards, which gives point to what otherwise might become dull routine.

XIII

Undirected Reading

You have finally become a literary reader when you are able to choose books for yourself and read them with pleasure without direction from anyone else.

Undirected reading includes what used to be called "silent reading," when children are required to read uninterruptedly to themselves from a book, usually of their own choice. At best this follows on from browsing.

When undirected reading time is a regular provision throughout a child's school career, right up through high school, a solid foundation is gradually laid down of reading skill and enjoyment on which directed reading — the close study of certain "key" texts by the class led by the teacher — can be built.

Some years ago a teacher, John Werner, neatly summarized the arguments in favor of undirected reading thus:

1. Each pupil must be given the opportunity to read at his own speed material of a difficulty suited to him. Such reading requires frequent practice.

2. No teacher can estimate which book will satisfy the intellectual and emotional needs of the individual. Therefore many books must be tried.

3. Such reading cannot be left to the pupil's leisure time. Many children come from homes where serious reading is simply not part of the way of life; T.V., with all its advantages, has surely cut down the incentive to acquire the habit of reading seriously where this is not already part of the accepted social pattern.

4. The teacher should not always be involved in the response to a book. Emotional blocks to reading can be formed by an unsatisfactory relationship with a teacher. With classes the size that they are it is not always possible for him to detect the

problems soon enough. In any case, a previous teacher may have left him with the legacy of an unsatisfactory attitude to reading. Much "free" writing in fact gives the teacher the response he wants. Response to teacher-dominated reading carries the same danger.

5. A teacher cannot keep up with all the books from which a child's reading should be selected. If directed reading is alone encouraged, the class will merely reflect the taste of the teacher rather than evolve their own.

6. If a child is reading only trash, then this fact should be taken into account and dealt with in English lessons. [See Chapter nine, "Worrying about the Rubbish."]

7. Many of our major authors (Dickens and Wells for example) were nourished on an early diet of wide, random reading, and in our own time, the number of outstanding young authors who are writing in spite of rather than because of classroom education is not inconsiderable. The outstanding example is Alan Sillitoe, who started writing seriously only after reading undisturbed during a lengthy spell in hospital.

8. The child must learn to discriminate for himself. If a pupil is allowed to accept or reject, he himself will demand higher standards in reading material far sooner than if his teacher attempts to tell him what is good and what is bad.*

How should undirected reading lessons be conducted? What are the snags and problems?

I have stressed, and Werner's summary emphasizes, that such sessions must be regular and frequent — at least one a week. But they cannot be imposed on children who are not used to them without some preparation. Essentially, they must be presented as pleasurable times to be looked forward to. And it is best if everyone comes prepared, knowing what they want to read. Classes which are not accustomed to the practice will need weaning. A good idea is to read aloud for a part of each session because this is a corporate activity that will settle them down and tune their imaginations to the right frequency. For the rest of the session they can be told to read their own books silently, and this

*John Werner, *The Practice of English Teaching*, Graham Owens and Michael Marland, eds. (London: Blackie, 1970) p. 161.

part of the session can gradually be lengthened as the children grow in stamina and appetite.

In fact only very avid readers will ever settle to silent reading immediately on arrival from some different activity. A few minutes spent with teacher and pupils talking about books (new ones just in from the supplier, for example, or those people have read and want to recommend to others) or any book-related topic treated conversationally in a by-the-way fashion serves the double purpose of preparing the right set of mind while at the same time attracting attention to books that might be enjoyed. This is really a "bridge passage" leading smoothly from one occupation — science, or P.E. or maths, etc. — to literary reading.

Younger and less skilled children are, of course, unable to sustain silent reading for very long, and younger children especially enjoy talking to themselves while they look at a book. But more mature readers can be expected to go on for full sessions without flagging, a point that most children should reach by ten years old. Others will need help in developing stamina and concentration by having rest times when what they are reading can be discussed. This gives them time to gather their energies again.

Once the silent reading session is accepted then an understanding should also be reached that at these times classmates should not be interrupted, either for idle chatter or for sharing responses.

This last is tricky. It is entirely natural for children to want to tell their friends about something they enjoy, and it is essential that this desire be given an outlet. If, however, this is allowed free play then the "silent" reading is soon silent no longer, and whether children want to share their friends' reactions or not, they are disturbed by the noise of those who do. The most satisfactory answer to the difficulty is to make it a matter of routine that before the end of each session, time is allowed for swopping excitements, but that during the reading time these must be contained as a simple courtesy in recognition of other people's right to read undisturbed. Once established, a look, a nod, or a warning sign from the teacher is usually enough to remind forgetful children of the accepted mode of behavior and to prevent distractions.

Reaching such a point of ease may be a long haul with some children and with classes who have unfavorable sets inbuilt from past bad teaching or lack of such experience. But this is the goal to be aimed for, and once attained it is a source from which other things flow — sessions of reading aloud to each other in small groups, and discussion or writing, drama or anthology programs based on books read and in spontaneous response, begin to blur the line that seems, as I write of it here, to separate undirected reading from other activities. In practice, once the barriers are broken down in children antagonistic to reading, everything blends into the flux of a whole experience split into bits only by the dictates of a school timetable. The experience itself we can recognize is made up of that reading circle described in Chapter four:

1. selecting what to read;
2. the act of reading what has been selected;
3. expressing responses generated by the reading;
4. being thus led on to make further selections in order to enjoy the pleasure of reading again.

Clearly, browsing about to find one's own preferences, and reading without intervention from others unless it is asked for are two major parts in that whole scheme. It is the teacher's job to make sure they are provided for in school.

PART FOUR

Response

XIV

Talking about Literature

The most usual response when people have enjoyed reading a book is for them to talk about it with their friends. They want to share the experience, want to sort out what it means. The study of literature with children is based on this kind of talk; indeed, it is the basis of all literary criticism, formal and informal.

How can we use such talk, and develop it so that people — adults as well as children — grow in their enjoyment and appreciation of literature? In order to answer that question we must begin by examining how this kind of talk "works."

SHARING

What people talk about as they share their pleasure in reading a particular book can be grouped under three headings.

Sharing enthusiasms. We tend to begin by communicating the fact of our pleasure. ("I've just finished reading this marvelous book . . . ," "Have you read ———— ? Didn't you enjoy it?") Having established our attitude we tend to continue by picking out aspects of the book we particularly liked. In this way we often find ourselves talking about the story (the what-happened-next element), the characters, the style (diction, images, the authorial manner), the ideas raised by the story, the author, this book compared with other books like it.

Sharing puzzles. Very soon we bring into the conversation aspects of the book which have puzzled us and, by discussing them, try to sort out what we think was meant. We ask each other questions like, "What do you think about the scene in which . . .?," "What was all that talk about between the husband and wife after they split up?," "Why do you think the author did this or that . . . ?" Often we "hide" our puzzlement behind comments like, "I didn't like the way the story ended, did you?" or "I wasn't convinced by the husband as a character . . ." By hearing what other people have to say, and by listening to what we say for ourselves as the talk progresses (for we often surprise ourselves by saying things we did not know we thought till we said them), we enlarge our understanding both of the book itself and our attitude to it.

Sharing connections. The result of sharing enthusiasms (and lack of enthusiasms) and of sharing puzzles is that we begin to see more clearly and with greater force what the book meant to us personally, and discover what it meant to other people, which may be something quite different from the connection it made with ourselves. We also begin to see how this fiction matches life as we know it or as it might be. In other words, we match the world of the book against the world we live in.

These three features in the talk are not, of course, gone through in order, as if they were items on an agenda. They are mixed up as the talk meanders about, apparently without conscious pattern. In fact the talk is guided by immediate need: by the need of the participants to express satisfactions, or dissatisfactions, the need to articulate new thoughts, the need to "bring out" from ourselves disturbing elements provoked by the book so that we can externalize them — hold them out, so to speak, where we can look at them and gain control of them. Talking about literature is a form of shared contemplation, a means by which we give consideration to the thoughts and emotions stimulated by the object of the book and the text it communicates to us — the imaginatively controlled messages sent from the author.

The way talk is used to do this can be expressed thus:

TALK ABOUT THE BOOK AND ME

Retelling the narrative. It is very noticeable that a great deal of book-talk begins with a statement of enthusiasm and proceeds at once to a retelling, in the reader's own words, of parts of the story: "I've just read this amazing book. It's about a man who . . ." So strong is the need to recreate the story in our own words that when two friends discover they have both read and enjoyed the same book their talk often consists simply of sharing retellings: "I especially liked that part where. . . . ," "Yes, so did I. And the scene in which. . . ." And so on as they relive and share their pleasure, just as they might relive a happy holiday together by telling each other about their experiences. When children talk among themselves this kind of talk is their normal and natural mode.

A striking feature of this narrative retelling is that it is highly selective. Very few people retell the whole story with all the incidents arranged as they are in the book. And quite frequently details, sometimes significant details that determine the nature of the original story, are changed in the retelling. Does this happen simply because the reader has forgotten the original, or because there is an unconscious desire to change the story to suit the reader's own preference? Of course we misremember details, and sometimes we do subconsciously change stories to suit our own ends. But from the observer's point of view — someone witnessing the talk from outside the conversation — it does not matter why the changes happen. What is often clear — and especially so with children — is why particular scenes are the ones a reader chooses to retell and the reasons why certain details are changed. In other words, as teachers of literature we soon discover that book-talk tells us as much about the reader as it does about the book, as indeed we all soon realize that critics tell us as much about themselves in their critical writings as they do about the objects of their criticism.

Some people have used this feature of response as a way of helping them deal with children therapeutically. Bruno Bettelheim provides a number of examples of his use of fairy tales with disturbed teenagers in his book *The Uses of Enchantment*, and there are numerous articles to be read about "bibliotherapy." Whatever the merits of such practice, I must make it clear that in my view the teaching of literature has nothing to do with it. The good teacher of literature concentrates all his and his pupils' attention on *the work*: the work which is the literature itself, and the work of reaching a deeper and more aware appreciation of the literature. The whole point, it seems to me, of the value of literature is that it achieves its most profound effects through a wholly private relationship between the reader-in-the-book and the author-in-the-book. If the reader wishes to externalize that relationship, wishes to "open it up" to another reader, this will happen best as an act of free choice, and through talk which is guided by a mutual focus on the literary work itself.

If the talk proceeds beyond retelling the narrative, it tends to move into conversation about the reader, sparked off by features in the book. A scene involving the book's protagonist and a snowfall, for example, might lead to talk about the reader's experience of snow. This is a very simple and obvious connection of ideas: the book deals with an event; this sparks off a memory or concern of the reader, who then goes on to rework his own experience or his concern. When this track is followed, the conversation very quickly drifts away from the book and becomes gossip about ourselves. Nothing wrong in this, when we are engaged in ordinary, everyday informal chat. But it is not a direction a teacher wants to encourage at times when literary exploration is the object of the talk. Though we should bear in mind that all talk needs moments of relaxation, when we forget the main topic for a short time while our minds "take a breather" and we recoup our energy. Children need these distractions during sessions of book-talk. They present the teacher with plenty of opportunities for "red herrings," which they can be allowed to follow when the teacher judges the time is right. Similarly it is part of a teacher's skill to be able to draw the conversation back to concentrated book-talk without being abrupt or obvious about it, so that the rhythm and easy flow is maintained.

There is another track the talk can follow. Not just talk about me-as-me — gossip that moves away from any consideration of the book. But talk about me-and-the-book. Generally speaking, this is about the matching of the reader, as a person, against the book. Crudely put, we discuss whether we are like the characters in the book, whether our life is like their lives, and so on. The book becomes a sampler, a pattern against which we can compare what we are.

In either case — me-as-me or me-and-the-book — we are making use of the book for our own ends. Our reading has become self-focused. We are finding out what we are and what the book can tell us about ourselves rather than trying to discover what the author and the book are trying to say to us regardless of any particular application to ourselves.

A work of literature is contained in a book which is itself an object — ink on paper bound together as pages — as well as being words (and sometimes pictures too) that create patterns of meaning.

A reader's experience of a book is influenced by both the book-object itself, and by the patterns of meaning created quite intangibly in the reader's head. What we must recognize is that this "text," this construct of object and meaning-pattern, lives only within the reader's imagination and is a constantly changing gestalt. We cannot take it out and look at it, or show it to someone else. Even as we try to describe it, it changes. Each time we talk about a book we discover that our sense of it, our ideas about it, our understanding of what it is and means, even the details we remember, have changed and shifted and come to us in different arrangements, different patterns. During our reading our idea of the book, its gestalt, changes because new information is added — new scenes, more details about the characters, and so on. After a reading, the patterns go on shifting according to our memory, our recall of the information, and whatever personal needs we have at that time and which particular features of the book "speak to."

The text changes too as other people's responses are added to our own. Sometimes this exchange can be sufficient to reshape our reaction from one of dislike and puzzlement to liking and understanding. I struggled with Flann O'Brien's At Swim-Two-Birds three or four times, never getting beyond the first fifty pages or so, until I read John Wain's critical essay in his book A House for the Truth, after which the novel suddenly seemed manageable, and I read it with great pleasure. A fine example of good criticism, and good literary teaching, the kind which helps us all read with more enjoyment and understanding what our teachers or our critics have found to be of value. But this is not just a matter of teachers and critics; we can all do the same for each other, provided we have discovered how to talk in a way that gets beyond the self-focusing use of literature.

So talk that concentrates on the text as Text — on the patterns created in our imaginations by our reading — is an attempt to discover the work of literature itself. This kind of talk is made up of all the other kinds discussed so far, but goes beyond them. And paradoxically the deeper we search for the Text, the more we discover about ourselves. In the same way that people who climb Everest or sail alone around the world tell us that in the very act of concentration on a work so difficult and dangerous they discover far more than ever before about themselves.

Equally of course such concentration very quickly tests the richness of a Text. Those that lack density, that possess little richness and have little to say, soon seem arid, not worth the effort. We quickly lose interest, give them perhaps one reading and never think of them again. Nor has this richness, this density, necessarily to do with complexity and great length. Aesop's Fables, like the parables of the New Testament in the Christian Bible, are, as literary structures, quite simple and short. Yet they constantly occupy people's attention because they reward frequent readings with fresh insights. They never pale; and they are memorable.

Clearly, then, in respect of literary education this last kind of talk is the kind we most want children to engage in. What we must not assume, however, is that the right thing to do with children or anyone else is to engage them like this straightaway, without any kind of preparation. There is a critical path that may be followed which takes account of what people are as people — as well as what they are as readers. This path we shall explore soon. But before that we should consider another way of sorting out the nature of book-talk that helps make the process clearer still.

LEVELS OF RESPONSE

In 1966 a conference of British and American teachers met at Dartmouth College, New Hampshire, to discuss literature and children. Their report included a useful analysis of the four "levels of response" which they noted as "emerging in sequence" as children grow as readers. The entire report is important to our subject and can be found reprinted in *The Cool Web: Patterns of Children's Reading*, edited by Margaret Meek, Aidan Warlow, and Griselda Barton.*

These *levels* are in part just another way of expressing what I have already said, but they also make up a statement of reading development that can be applied in two ways. It is a statement about the track children follow as they grow into literary readers; it is also a statement of the elements that make up a reading of any work of literature by a literary person. In other words, during every reading a literary reader re-experiences his literary growth.

Here are the four levels identified by the Dartmouth conference:

Sound. The report says, "When children bounce on mother's knee to a song or a nursery rhyme, when they join in the chorus, when they chant 'maximum capacity' round the room, and maybe when they chuckle at special words, names, and puns, they are responding to the texture and rhythm of sounds. Such overt actions seem to be both elements of their enjoyment and signs of it."†

I have been suggesting throughout this book that the element of sound — what I have called "the drama of print" — is an important pleasure-giving element in all literary reading. Frequently people who reject literature, those who find no value in reading it, turn out to be people who cannot "hear" a text as they read it silently for themselves. They cannot hear the dialogue as people talking; cannot, as Richard Hoggart puts it, "shift the gears" of their reading to suit the dramatic needs of the text —

---

*Margaret Meek and others, eds., *The Cool Web: Patterns of Children's Reading* (London: The Bodley Head, 1977; New York: Atheneum, 1978) pp. 379-392.
†Ibid, p. 380.

the needs of pacing and of "voice."

To re-emphasize a point that cannot be over-emphasized: reading aloud to children of all ages is vital, if for no other reason, because this is the way we learn how to turn cold print into a dramatic enactment in the theater of our imagination.

Event. The rhythm of sound makes a pattern. The reader-hearer expects that pattern to develop in a certain way, which it may or may not do, but in either case we take pleasure both in the expectation and in the actual outcome. Similarly, the form of the story or poem creates a pattern of events based on character and action and motive (even a lyric poem has a sayer, is an event, and has a reason-for-being, and is, in this sense, a story). As we read, these two — sound and event — build up expectations about their resolutions, which may be satisfied in predictable or in unexpected ways.

Our reading may fix all its attention on this element, in which case, as many readers do, we concentrate on the *what-happens-next* part of the narrative. And when we come to talk about our reading we focus all our talk on retelling the story. As the Dartmouth Report puts it in providing an example, "When a child corrects a storyteller and wants the story word perfect, he is asking for a confirmation of the pattern (in one respect or the other). At a later stage he may make up topsy-turvy stories with reversals of the pattern; finally he will improvise and impose his own."*

(Which, by the way, tells us one of the reasons why nonsense verse and story is so important, especially at about the time when children are learning to read for themselves. They have just learned the "rules," and nonsense verse provides the enormous pleasure of breaking the rules and finding how far they can be stretched before they snap.)

Role. "In free play or classroom drama," the Dartmouth Report says, "children take up the roles of characters in their stories, or perhaps continue the role playing that the story involved them in: 'I'm Jack and this is the beanstalk and you be the giant.'

*Ibid, p. 381.

Sometimes children will replay the story, sometimes reshape and improvise on it, perhaps relating the roles and the events more nearly to their own wishes."*

Everyone who has worked with children has seen this happen. But we should not think it happens only in children's play. Every reader experiences something like it as part of the experience of literature. Even the most sophisticated reader, while absorbed in reading, enjoys the sense of being a character, and the feeling of engaging in the events described, the emotions stimulated and the thoughts provoked. The experience, in other words, of being "inside" the book, a participator (with the author and the characters) in the life of the alternative world. Even — to try and show how subtle this can be — when we are not "being" one of the characters there is always the strange magic of the voice in our heads. Who is this speaking? Who is it that I hear telling this story, speaking this poem? It is not me, for I did not write the words. Yet it is not the author, either, whose voice I probably have never heard. And yet each book has its own voice, its own speaker. And, though part of me knows that voice is other than mine, another part — the part which is absorbed in the book — feels that it is "the voice," that it is creating the story, the poem, the play, as I read along. It is one of the most compelling aspects of literature, this sense of becoming the narrator, of taking on the personality who creates the work. It is also one of the least well understood.

In book-talk we try to replay the experience in the form of talk about *me-in-the-book*. We recount the parts which absorbed us utterly, which "convinced us," which made us feel that the alternative world was more vivid, more alive, more immediate, more "real," than our life outside the book. Those who are not literary readers have never learned to hear the drama of print, and because they cannot hear the drama they never become absorbed in the alternative world, and so never find that extraordinary pleasure that demands to be experienced time and time again, book after book. They see literary readers sitting "lost" in a book and cannot think what it is we find there.

*Ibid, p. 381.

When we have discovered this, our response enters the fourth level:

World. The Dartmouth Report: "While a story is being read aloud to a group a child may interpose: 'He's a funny boy' (about Jan in *The Silver Sword* [by Ian Serraillier] perhaps), and the group may begin to talk about his background, his relations with the other characters, etc." A new variety of talk develops to relate and organize elements of the world of that story or to relate the world of that story to a child's own world. It will tie in all the four kinds of response, giving some "new articulation."* Of course the same thing, the same kind of contemplation, can go on inside us as we read, and afterwards.

It is in this "new articulation" that the best value of literary reading and response lies. When it functions in us like this, literature gives us images to think with. It offers us entry into a vast complex of experience beyond and different from our own which adds to and illuminates anything we can ever hope to know through our own lives and beings. Thus in an attentive reader literature is expansive, visionary, challenging, subversive, in the true and best sense. It helps bring us to an awareness of the world and of our self in a way that could not possibly be achieved otherwise.

THE TEACHER OF LITERATURE

All too often in the teaching of literature, just as in the teaching of most other "subjects," teachers play the game, "Guess what's in my head." A text is read. The teacher poses questions about it. The pupils must find the answers the teacher is waiting to hear. Even when there is a possibility of more than one "correct" answer, the teacher frequently accepts only the one he is waiting for, pushing the others aside as "right but not what I'm after." This creates the impression that only the teacher's required answer is credit-worthy.

The study of literature is not best conducted in this fashion. Such a method literally misleads children into believing that

*Ibid, p. 381.

literature is really nothing but a very complicated and confusing comprehension test that bears no relation to anything they might think or feel for themselves. A university lecturer unwittingly put all this in a nutshell when she said to me during a discussion of her students' work, "I don't want to know their opinions of a book. I want to know they've learned what they are supposed to know." That attitude betrays a total ignorance of what literature and literary reading is about.

What should happen is this. A text is read (silently or aloud). Inevitably everyone involved experiences a variety of responses. These are reported, are shared, in a conversation which will follow the paths I have outlined in this chapter — or, to use the Dartmouth Report's language, will proceed through various levels. The teacher takes part in this sharing, reporting his own responses, but using his talk to help guide the conversation so that it is kept focused on the Text: on the literary work.

In part, therefore, the teacher is a reader among readers, an equal with his own contribution to make about the nature of the Text as he knows it. In part he is a chairperson, seeing that the talk is conducted in such a way that individual contributions are respected and that everyone gets a chance. In part he is a leader, responsible for guiding the talk so that everyone is helped to understand what it is that is being said about the book, and claimed for it. In this aspect of his work he is and needs to be more experienced, more knowledgeable, more skilled as a reader than his pupils.

All of which means that we must be in command of a critical method, an approach to literature and the discussion of it, which guides our work with child readers. This "Critical Blueprint" we will now explore.

XV

A Critical Blueprint

As we read in preparation for bringing a book to children we ask ourselves a number of questions which help clarify the nature of the book and the way we should mediate it to children. These questions may be asked as we read the book, or afterwards, as we contemplate the experience.

1. *What happened to me as I read?* We cannot read anything without experiencing many kinds of response. The boy who told his teacher, "This is the most boring book I have ever read" was simply reporting what had happened to him. In the same way we can note when we are absorbed, when not, when we are amused or saddened, when a character specially interested us, when a passage of writing held our attention for its own sake, and so on. In other words, it is possible when we have read a book, and even while we are in the act of reading it for the first time, to tell the story of our reading.

2. *Which features of the book caused my responses?* In telling the story of our reading, we can ask why we reacted as we did. What was it that "triggered" our responses? The causes may have four sources:

a. *The book-as-object.* In talking about our reading we tend to forget this influence. But the Text which lives in our imaginations — that gestalt we discussed earlier — is communicated to us through ink on pages bound as a book. So the book-object is a piece of sculpture which, like any piece of sculpture, can please or displease us, cause us to make this or that association. And this book-sculpture not only has shape and weight and texture as well as visual appeal, it also has a smell and is mobile — it can be open and closed (with more or less satisfaction in the way it does this) and be carried easily about with us. To children this aspect of a book is often of much more conscious importance than it is to many sophisticated adult readers. Think of infants, whose first response to a book is often to put as much of it as possible into their mouths; and for some time after infancy many children continue to regard books as they regard their toys, as objects to be played with and looked at rather than read. I can still remember the look and feel of the old-fashioned annuals that used to be produced at Christmas time. They were very fat, and large in format, and had extremely thick and what I now know to be coarse and cheap paper. But I loved them and was usually given at least three as Christmas presents. The first thing I did was pile them one on another and then sit on them while I looked at my other presents. Not until later in the day did I look at them as books.

Paperback publishers know how strong an influence the look and feel of a book can have in attracting or repelling buyers. They will often make visual appeals with the use of dramatic or sexual images that succeed in attracting buyers but are not so successful at representing the Text: as, Thomas Hardy's novels presented with nudes on the covers. Good book-selling, like good teaching, seeks to raise the right expectations in the potential reader, expectations which will be satisfied by the Text.

An example. I once gave *The Shrinking of Treehorn* by Florence Parry Heide to a group of elementary school teachers in England and asked them to commentate, rather in the manner of radio sports reporters, their reactions from the moment they began looking at the book. The British edition of *Treehorn* has a cover printed almost all over in a particular shade of light green. The first thing that happened was that a number of the group reacted strongly against that color. Some said it made them feel sick; one man hated it so much he decided he could not read the book and left the group. Talking about the expectations raised by the cover took well over half an hour. Some people said that the title and the drawing led them to expect a serious fantasy; very few expected anything like the witty and satiric story they discovered in the book. After three hours' talk we had not got beyond the third incident in the story — so many, so various, and so provocative of further thoughts and ideas, were the responses reported as the text was read aloud. And everything came into the conversation, from the quality of the paper, the kind of print, the way the words and pictures are handled, the nature of the illustrations themselves (considerable controversy on this point), as well as much discussion of the thematic material — adults and their relations with children, the view children have of adults, the nature of humor and the differences in child and adult humor, and so on.

The exercise was one of the most instructive, as well as entertaining, sessions of work with teachers and literature that I have ever taken part in; we all went away, I think, with a considerably changed attitude towards books-as-objects (and the influence on our reading of this aspect of literature), towards the potentials that lie in reportage-based discussion of our reading, and towards the value of this kind of talk in deepening and widening our understanding and the pleasure we take in literature.

In one respect in particular did we find such talk helpful. Prejudices of taste (or reading habits) are one of the biggest barriers against children's and adults' willingness to explore beyond the known and familiar. Finding ways of breaking these prejudices down and encouraging a willingness to explore is one of the literature teacher's most difficult tasks. Reading-reportage brings these prejudices to the surface and opens them to discussion not just by the teacher but by the reader's peers, so that the prejudices are tested and other possibilities placed against it.

But we have reached away from our immediate topic: which is that the book-object is a prime, but sometimes unrecognized, cause of our response to a literary work.

b. *Responses caused by the reader's personal history.* As we read our whole lives — our personal histories — are open to the book and can be engaged, can be brought to memory, by features in the book, coloring our reaction to the features that raised them. Thus, for example, any domestic death scene and espe-

cially any funeral scene in a story inevitably conjures in myself
memories of my childhood spent as the son of an undertaker.
I have to allow for this, to set my personal reactions against what
I can intellectually understand the book is actually trying to do.
Undoubtedly in Dickens's *Oliver Twist* we are meant to feel the
eerie terror of Oliver's first night spent with the coffins in the
undertaker's workshop, where he is made to sleep. But to me that
incident is amusing rather than frightening, while also pleasing
me because Dickens gets it so "right": the little details of the
shop and the coffins and the atmosphere of the place I recall
exactly; they match my experience, and so my reading at this
point enters the level of me-in-the-book rather than remaining at
the level of event. And, clearly, the text-intention is not one I
receive (fear, being appalled on Oliver's behalf at this dreadful
treatment of a young boy, the terrible sense of his loneliness,
and so on). Instead, the book at this point slips by me; I do not
feel, as I am intended to, but only know with my mind what is
intended.

More often than we realize, perhaps, we have to clear away
this kind of overlay from our personal history before we can
reach down to that fourth level, the text-as-Text. Again, talking
about our personal-history-based responses helps us discover them
and to move them aside so that we can focus on the features
that stirred our history. With children, the teacher's job is to
help clarify the difference between the experience offered by the
book, and the same experience known to the reader personally.

c. *Response caused by the reader's history as a reader.*   Just as
our personal lives are open to the book as we read so are our
histories as readers. In one sense, all books are made out of other
books and all our reading is dependent on all we have read
before. I mean that to some extent stories, poems, plays are like
games. They work according to certain rules the reader-players
agree to follow. One of the things we are trying to discover when
we begin reading a book is which set of rules this particular book
is going to follow. If we do not know that set of rules, the game
is confusing and difficult to understand, which in turn makes it
hard to enjoy. We will often then give up, lay the book aside and

look for another game, another book, which follows more familiar rules.

Stories in books, even when they seem extremely simple like stories for preschool infants, — in picturebooks such as John Burningham's *Mr. Gumpy's Outing*, Marie Hall Ets's *Play With Me*, Pat Hutchins's *Rosie's Walk*, Robert McCloskey's *Make Way for Ducklings* and Iris Schweitzer's *Hilda's Restful Chair* — are complicated in the "rules" they follow. In our English-based culture, for example, we start at the "front" of the book (some other cultures have their front at what we think of as the back). We "read" from the top of the left-hand page, working in horizontal lines across the page and line by line down the page, then begin again at the top of the right-hand page, and so on, before "turning over" and starting again at the top of the next left-hand page. There is therefore a basic "rule" — our books follow a left to right flow; and when we turn over there is the possibility of surprise. Picture books make use of these elements — and so teach very young children how a book works while entertaining them with pictures.

A book like *Rosie's Walk* by Pat Hutchins not only uses those rules, it breaks one of them in such a way that it adds a new excitement for a young reader who may have just learned how to handle a book. The way the rule is broken works so well because the author-artist has employed a fact of reading that we usually ignore — which is that as we turn over a page the first part of the next two pages we see is not the top left-hand page (where we must begin to read) but the right-hand page. So Hutchins arranges her story-drawings in such a way that as you turn over you first see Rosie, calmly going about her morning's walk apparently safely and happily, and it is only as your eye travels leftwards (the "wrong" way) across the page and into the left-hand page itself that you see the fox who is stalking the hen and trying to catch her. This in turn sends your eye traveling to the right — "reading" the pages — in order that you can confirm to yourself that what you now know to be true is in fact what is happening, and to dwell with ironic amusement on Rosie's apparently ignorant sanguinity. You also very much want to turn over to see what will happen next: Will Rosie be caught?

Will Fox miss again? And what this time will be the cause of his slapstick downfall? So *Rosie's Walk* both uses the basic conventions of reading and adds new ones at the same time, melding both into the one story. This is one of the reasons that always makes people think it a "classic" of picture book making.

Sometimes an author will deliberately play on previous reading knowledge in order to make a story. This happens in *Each Peach Pear Plum* by Janet and Allan Ahlberg, in which nursery rhymes and stories are brought together to provide characters in a new book. At its simplest level, the Ahlbergs offer children a game of I Spy. If the child reader has had the misfortune to have lived for three or four years without having heard the stories of Tom Thumb or Cinderella or the three bears, the book can still be read, the game still played, because the characters who are obviously the ones named can be found hidden in the pictures. But the child who has the advantage of being brought up enriched by hearing stories and reading books will have the added and much greater pleasure of playing the game, airing his knowledge, re-experiencing the pleasure of the nursery stories, and finding a whole new story based on those familiar tales and verses.

These are obvious and extremely simple examples. My point is that all literature, every example we can think of, depends for its existence on the tradition out of which it springs — even the most *avant* of the *avant-garde*. James Joyce's *Ulysses*, once thought to be so difficult that it could hardly be read at all by most people, now seems far more manageable and easy, because we have learned how it is made from a variety of different styles of writing, from newspaper journalism through advertising and film script to Joycean treatments of literary conventions associated with different historical periods in English literature, as well as its use of Homer's *Odyssey*.

The same thing happens, with less complexity perhaps, in children's literature. Betsy Byars's *The Eighteenth Emergency* depends in part for its impact and the significance of its thematic resolution on our knowing that in most stories about bullies the hero is nastily abused and then confronts the bully and soundly beats him at his own game, as Tom does in *Tom Brown's Schooldays* (where we find the archetype of all schoolboy heroes and bullies). Betsy Byars's hero, Mouse Fawley, is not at all nastily abused; he is simply threatened. When he eventually faces the bully, as we all know he will have to, the ensuing fight is far from the blood-and-guts affair the convention would predict. So our expectations are raised, not by Betsy Byars but by the literary convention in which her story is set, and then are surprised and changed by the outcome the author creates for little Mouse. So her story is not so much about bullying and coping with a bully as it is about fear itself being far more disabling and awful to endure than either its cause or its consequences. But Byars can only work out her story in this way with any satisfaction to the young reader because of the literary context out of which her story comes.

From *Huckleberry Finn* to *Catcher in the Rye*, from *Coral Island* to *The Lord of the Flies*, from *Aesop's Fables* to *Animal Farm*: we can all find family trees for dozens of books. Equally, after a few moments' thought and talk about books we have just read, we all discover the family tree of our own reading into which the new work fits — or find ourselves in the position of discovering a work that for us is "new" in major features. Children can often find themselves in this position, and at such times talking with an adult who can help them "fit" the new work into its context, and who can lead them to other books that belong to the same "tree" is of profound importance in their development as literary readers.

Indeed, when a book calls strongly on another book, and the reader lacks knowledge of the source, then part of the book's pleasure is lost. Talking about our reading with a group of other people allows us to explore that element quickly, helps us sort it out, and encourages us to re-read the book in order to obtain the missed enjoyment.

d. *Response caused by the Text alone.* A book may also of course provoke responses based primarily on the text itself rather than on intrusions from our personal and reading histories. The accumulation of text detail can be so effective that the reader feels, or is provoked to thought, in a way guided by the author. The selection of details to tell the reader, as well as those not to include, is part of the skill of storytelling and writing. Arranging these details in such a way that a desired effect is achieved in the reader is another part. Thus in E. B. White's *Charlotte's Web* the gradual accumulation of details that make the spider attractive, even admired and liked as a character, and that build up a sense of her relationship with the pig enables us to feel sad at Charlotte's death, and to feel that it is a sacrificial and heroic one. Without that preparation the death would have been insignificant because we normally do not feel human sympathy for spiders. Children's responses to bears in a story are quite different. In real life, bears are dangerous and rather terrifying. In literature, perhaps because of the influence of stories like *Winnie the Pooh* and *Paddington Bear*, they are often so sentimentalized that an author who tried to treat one in a story as a villain would have a difficult job; children might actually object — a protest society for bears. Certainly many children's histories-as-readers would cause one of those prejudicial barriers of the kind we discussed earlier.

Our talk about what happened to us as we read will inevitably lead therefore to a discussion of text-based details, and the author's storytelling tactics, in order for us to explain why we felt and thought as we did. Or rather, it inevitably will if the teacher-guide subtly leads the conversation through those other "levels," those other me-as-me responses on which book-talk so often gets stuck. And this text-based talk reveals to us how the book "works" — the kind of literature we are dealing with. In other words, we slowly find out how this piece of literature wants to be read: what it wants the reader to bring to the reading: what it is this author is saying to us through the book. And so we finally move ourselves out of the focus and give all our attention to the book itself.

None of this is ever as schematic and neatly arranged, step-by-step, as my discussion of it here makes it seem. Sometimes, however hard we try in our book-talk, people's personally-based responses will so override everything else that in their cases this book or that is simply one they cannot — yet, for nothing about literary reading is ever permanent or finished — enjoy or feel sympathy for.

An important thing to keep in mind as we try to help children develop into thoughtful, mature literary readers is that being able to sort out our responses, and being able to trace their source, is formative in that development.

3. *What does this book ask of readers if they are to enjoy what it offers and discover the Text's potentialities?*

Some books, like Roald Dahl's *Danny: The Champion of the World*, are written with the reader in mind. They go out of their way to make their meaning plain, and to achieve a level of language and simplicity of structure the writer assumes most of his intended readers will feel at home with. Other authors, like Virginia Hamilton for example, are far less reader-conscious. They make demands which the reader must meet to enjoy the work. Sorting out what a reader must bring to a particular book helps us discover the elements a teacher may have to mediate to children, and which a teacher will want to bring out in talk about that book. (In my essay "The Reader in the Book," included in *The Signal Approach to Children's Books** I have explored in more detail this aspect of reading.)

Skilled professionals who have had some training in academic criticism will know how to tackle a text in this way. Others need only follow their reading noses and listen to what other readers say about a book, following the tracks I have outlined here. If we keep asking ourselves "What features of the story/poem/play impress me?" and "What is it that makes me think and feel as I do — why am I impressed?," then the text will in any case slowly reveal itself. We are all, from the time of our birth, possessed of a facility for criticism, just as we are all possessed of a facility for language. And as every teacher knows, children are keenly critical of what they read. The difference between naïve readers (whether adult or child) and sophisticated

---

*Aidan Chambers, "The Reader in the Book," *The Signal Approach to Children's Books*, Nancy Chambers, ed. (London: Kestrel, 1980; Metuchen, N. J.: Scarecrow Press, 1981) pp. 250-275.

readers (whether adult or child) is that the naïve reader has not learned how to sort out the nature and source of his responses and has not acquired a language in which to express his criticism.

One of the things a good teacher can do is listen to what children say and perceive the critical content couched in child language, which the teacher can then articulate again in a way that clarifies what the child means and, at the same time, teaches him how to say what he means. An example. After he had read some of the novels of Arthur Ransome, I asked ten-year-old William whether he did not find them rather long and perhaps a little "slow" (I meant lacking in actionful plots). William thought for a while and then said, "Arthur Ransome is the sort of writer you enjoy most after you have finished reading him." There was no other way that William could just then express the understanding he had clearly reached that some books are so difficult to read (when you first read them, at any rate), and so complex in their patterns, that it is only after you have finished them and can see them whole, and have time to think them through and sort out what you have felt and thought as you were reading, that you begin to feel strong pleasure. I would suggest this is true of almost all the great works of literature. The first time you read them they are often hard work, and the returns of pleasure are delayed until you are familiar with them and the way they "work." Had William said what he did as part of a formal book-talk session, my problem would have been to know how to expand what he said so that he and the other children could become aware of that truth about literature, without at the same time spoiling William's pleasure in reading Ransome, or pushing the discussion beyond the straightforword point William had raised.

Children's lack of sufficient book knowledge — lack of reading experience — makes it difficult sometimes for them to find useful comparisons that help them explain what they mean. And again, this is a point at which the teacher may need to intervene to provide examples. Which brings us back to the fact that books are made out of other books; that there is a family tree to which each book belongs.

Other things cause children to stumble as they try to sort

out their responses. Too many words in the text may be strange to them. The subject matter may be so far outside their experience that they have few personal reference points to help them understand what the book is doing and why this is important. The narrative may be unfamiliar in its structure so that they are unsure about the way different elements of the story fit together. To repeat a previous point: literary reading depends on the reader finding enough that is familiar to feel at home, but enough of the unexpected and unfamiliar to feel surprised, excited, interested.

Getting children to talk together, led by a literate adult, helps them sort out these problems and to learn from each other. They also learn that a book can be read in a number of different ways. Jane Austen's novels, for example, are often read simply as historical romance stories. The fact that they are satiric, are masterpieces of character drawing, are fascinating as portraits of a particular society at a particular time drawn by someone with a sharp eye for detail and an extraordinary control of language: all these things may be ignored. Perhaps only through talk in which all these elements of Austen's work are explored by people who happened to have enjoyed them for themselves will a naïve reader, who happens to have noticed only the romantic story, find out how much more there is to enjoy.

4. *Why is this book worth my own and children's time and attention?*
If we have worked our way through the previous questions, the answers to this one will be obvious. They may have to do with qualities inherent in the book itself. But they may also have to do with the needs of the children we have in mind. If we are faced with children who lack reading experience, whose reading stamina is weak, and who are reluctant to read very much for themselves, we are likely to present them with a sequence of shorter, very directly told, and uncomplicatedly structured books, rather than with denser and more subtle texts. We will be wanting to build up their confidence, provide them with repeated experiences of reading pleasure that confirm the worth of the activity, and so on. This is simply a matter of beginning where

children are and then, by the way we deal with their responses to what they have enjoyed reading, of finding ways and books that lead them on, of widening the range and scope of their choices and understanding. Very little in literary education is clear cut, but we can always be sure of the reasons why we offer a particular book to particular children, whether these be literary reasons or extra-literary ones, whether book-focused or reader-focused.

5. *Which would be the most appropriate ways of introducing this book to the children I have in mind?*

I am not thinking here of those "indirect methods" by which we bring books to children's attention: displays, for example, bulletin boards where children post their own reviews, and so on. Rather I have in mind methods by which we present books in a "direct," teacher-to-child way. These include:

"Have you read this?" sessions, in which we tell children about a book and what we think is enjoyable in it;

reading aloud extracts, especially the opening chapter, in order to get the book started and create an "appetite" for the story (many children find it much harder to get into a new book by an author they have never read before than they do to get into a new book by an author already familiar to them);

reading the whole book at one sitting (as it is possible to do with *The Shrinking of Treehorn* to, say, nine-year-olds), or reading it in serial episodes spread over a number of days (as might be done with *The Eighteenth Emergency* to, say, ten-year-olds);

showing audio-visual material, such as Weston Woods films about an author or a book; various TV programs dealing with children's books can be used to stimulate interest too;

a visit from the author and/or illustrator;

a close reading, which begins with a session in which the book is introduced and perhaps the opening chapter or chapters read; this followed by either a serial reading or the children reading the book for themselves silently; after which the teacher leads a discussion of the book and the children's responses to it — book-talk of the kind discussed earlier; (an essential of this approach, of course, is that every child has a copy of the book).

The choice of approach will depend on a judgment about what would most suit the book and the children's needs in relation to it. There are no rules about introducing any book; everything depends on the adult's skill and sensitivity.

6. *What do I know of the background to this book — about its author, or how it came to be written, or the place where it is set, and so on — that might interest the children and stimulate their desire to read?*

Just as adults do, children like to know the story behind a story. It is worthwhile therefore keeping to hand, as part of the staff reference collection, a selection of the kind of book which gives biographies of authors and illustrators* and to build up a file of articles culled from journals and other sources that cover authors and books and aspects of literature that are useful for this purpose. Sometimes children like keeping their own personal or class files about authors, and bulletin board displays about authors made by children after they have enjoyed a book or when they get hooked on a particular author are a useful channel for response and act as a stimulus to other children to read those books and authors too. (The bulletin boards can include short biographies written by children or obtained from publishers' publicity departments, photographs of the authors, children's reviews, comments, artworks relating to the books, letters written to the authors and received back in reply.) Of course, when interest is very strong the natural outcome is an author-visit.

7. *Are there books by the same author, or by other authors, which relate to this one and which the children have already read, or perhaps ought to read before reading this one? And are there books which follow on naturally from this one?*

*For example, the *Something About the Author* series (Gale Research Co.); *Twentieth Century Children's Writers* (Macmillan Press, Ltd., London; St. Martin's Press, New York); the *Illustrators of Children's Books* series (The Horn Book).

No book, as we have seen, exists on its own. No book is ever enough on its own. All books have close relations in other books. Literary reading is not about one book but about the multiplicity of ideas, the richness of experience, the density of images, the constantly renewing sustenance we receive from the thoughtful reading of many books. The skilled teacher therefore tries to place every book given to children in the context of other books.

As an example of both the relatedness of books, and how literature teaching can and perhaps should make use of this with children in close-reading study, Professor Jon Stott gave the following list in a useful article, "Criticism and the Teaching of Stories to Children" printed in *Signal* 32, May 1980. Stott was especially interested in the frequent use of the enclosed garden in fiction both for children and adults and wanted to explore this with a class of seven-year-olds in ways they could enjoy and which would increase their understanding and literary consciousness. The books listed below are in the order used in Stott's program of work — that is, the order of their relatedness, one book, in a sense, being a preparation for the next, the aim being to lead to *The Secret Garden* itself.

GAIL HALEY: *A Story, A Story* (U.S., Atheneum; U.K., Methuen)

LEO LIONNI: *Frederick* (U.S., Pantheon; U.K., Abelard)

TARO YASHIMA: *Crow Boy* (U.S., Viking)

HANS ANDERSEN: *Thumbelina* (U.S., Scribner)

ELIZABETH CLEAVER: *The Mountain Goats of Temlahem* (U.S., Oxford)

GERALD MCDERMOTT: *Arrow to the Sun* (U.S., Viking; U.K., Kestrel)

MARIA CAMPBELL: *Little Badger and the Fire Spirit* (Canada, McClelland & Stewart)

LEO & DIANE DILLON, [il.]: *Why Mosquitoes Buzz in People's Ears* (U.S., Dial)

NONNY HOGROGIAN: *One Fine Day* (U.S., Macmillan; U.K., Hamish Hamilton)

BARBARA COONEY, [il.]: *Chanticleer and the Fox* (U.S., Crowell; U.K., Kestrel)

MARJORIE FLACK: *The Story about Ping* (U.S., Viking; U.K., Bodley Head)

BEATRIX POTTER: *The Tale of Peter Rabbit* (U.K. and U.S., Warne)

MAURICE SENDAK: *Where the Wild Things Are* (U.S., Harper & Row; U.K., Bodley Head)

MORDECAI RICHLER: *Jacob Two-Two Meets the Hooded Fang* (U.S., Random House; U.K., Deutsch)

LESLIE BROOKE: *Johnny Crow's Garden* (U.K. and U.S., Warne)

FRANCES HODGSON BURNETT: *The Secret Garden* (U.S., Lippincott; U.K., Heinemann)

VIRGINIA LEE BURTON: *The Little House* (U.S., Houghton Mifflin; U.K., Faber)

Stott's program is a demanding one for children of the age he was teaching. But, as his article tries to make clear, such a developed approach is entirely possible with any age-group, after five, without loss of reading pleasure provided that the books chosen and the discussion of them are appropriate to the particular children involved.

Let Professor Stott explain:

During the last three years, my approach has taken focus and I have developed what is, in essence, a literature curriculum for Grade Two (seven- and eight-year-old) children. The groups I've been working with have ranged in size from twenty to twenty-five pupils and have generally been composed of children of Anglo-European heritage, although there have been some with native American or African background. Some have professional parents, several of whom are on the faculty of the University of Alberta. There is a very low percentage of single-parent families.

My goal is a simple one: to enhance the children's enjoyment of the stories we share by increasing their understanding of them. To achieve my end, I must always keep in mind the fact that much of the meaning of a story is implicit in its visual and verbal details and that the children are just now reaching an age at which they can approach stories in a manner that is not completely literal. To develop in them an ability to see implicit meanings and patterns, however, one must proceed slowly, cautiously, and delicately, and must be aware of the many pitfalls surrounding such an approach. The greatest challenge I faced was discovering the most effective means of developing the children's interest and understanding.

A great deal of my work involved preparation. First, I assessed the children, considering what boys and girls of their age and backgrounds could be expected to comprehend. (I have found that they can often respond at a level higher than many people might expect and that children of different backgrounds have very similar responses to the same stories or types of stories.) Second, I chose specific books appropriate to the age level and the specific groups. The majority of works chosen were picture books, it having been my experience that at this age most children can more easily examine visual details, notice the implications of them, and see the patterns they form. To the works selected, I applied the critical and analytical techniques which enabled me to understand them on an adult level and then asked myself which of the aspects I had discovered could be made accessible to the children and would be useful in helping them toward fuller understanding and appreciation of the book in question. The end result of this stage was a list of seventeen titles (see above), which served as the teaching core for the year's literature program.

The third preparatory stage was perhaps the most difficult, but certainly the most important: placing the stories in a sequence so that each story shared a common element (theme, character type, artistic technique) with those stories immediately preceding and following it and so that stories studied earlier would help the children develop skills of analysis which would facilitate their understanding and enjoyment of more difficult but similar works studied later in the year. I began with Gail Haley's A Story, A Story, the first of three pourquoi books we were to look at, and the first of several stories which included trickster figures and individuals who were tested. Ananse, who brings stories to his people, provided a lead in to Leo Lionni's Frederick, who tells stories and poems to his fellow winterbound mice. It might be said that I was following the directive of the poet Robert Frost, who once wrote that "a poem is best read in the light of all the other poems ever written. We read A the better to read B (we have to start somewhere, we may get very little out of A). We read B the better to read C, C the better to read D, D the better to go back and get something more out of A."

When I met the children, I had to work to avoid making two mistakes which are inherent in the approach and to which I as a university professor am particularly prone: an adult-level discussion and analytical overkill. (More than once during my first years in elementary schools, children said, "Can't we stop talking and read more of the story?" Discussion had become "disgust-ion" and the reading of the stories wasn't fun for the children.) It was important that the seventeen stories should form only a small portion of the children's literature program. Accordingly, their teacher read them other (and, when possible, related) stories, but for pleasure only; they took frequent trips to the school library; and they were given regular silent reading periods. Children's authors visiting the region were invited to come to the school to meet the class.

In order to make my twice-weekly half-hour visits to the class more relaxing and, I hoped, more enjoyable, the teacher and I designed a special area the children called "the story-corner." The walls were decorated with a map of the world, on to appropriate places of which the children pinned flags bearing the titles of the books; an author tree, on to which they pasted photographs of the authors; and cardboard plaques displaying names of important characters. While I generally read the stories, I occasionally used filmstrips, storyboards, or movies for variety. Once, I showed a videotape in which I was reading the story to another group.

The analysis, which I believe to be so important, took no more than five minutes of each half-hour period. I wished the children to see how visual and/or verbal details and the relationship between details contributed to the development of action, mood, and character. I focused on only one aspect for each book: for example, the way the position of the hero on the page in Lionni's Frederick indicated the mouse's status among his fellows. I showed that the increasing amounts of grey and brown in the pictures reflected the feeling of unhappiness and abandonment felt by the title character of Virginia Lee Burton's The Little House and how the smallness of Chibi in the early pictures of Taro Yashima's Crow Boy paralleled his role in the school. I pointed out one or two pictures in each book to illustrate my points and then invited the children to find similar aspects in other pictures. The children began to recognize that the stories implicitly conveyed emotions and qualities of character, ones they themselves were familiar with. A few public symbols were also drawn to their attention: the corn symbols in *Arrow to the Sun* and the relationship between weather and human emotions in *Jacob Two-Two Meets the Hooded Fang*. Some guidance on my part was used to lead to awareness and further discussion; however, the children were neither quizzed nor tested.

I introduced these three books [*The Tale of Peter Rabbit, Johnny Crow's Garden*, and *The Secret Garden*] into the curriculum because I wished to develop in the students an awareness of the garden as a significant setting and, in reading *The Secret Garden*, to have them trace the parallels between the development of the characters of Mary and Colin and the reclamation of the garden. We began reading the books in late February, after we had been meeting together for nearly six months. Up to this time, we had looked at fourteen stories, one of them, Mordecai Richler's *Jacob Two-Two Meets the Hooded Fang*, a short novel. The children had become fairly proficient in seeing how visual and/or verbal details formed patterns revealing character development. In effect, they had become aware of story structure.

The Tale of Peter Rabbit had been introduced earlier in the year so that when we returned to it the children knew it well. Our focus this time was on Mr. McGregor's garden, and the children and I examined how that setting represented a private and forbidden area. I asked why Mr. McGregor had a fence around the garden and whether or not Peter needed to go there for food. During the discussion, we considered other settings, both those in stories we'd read together and those in other stories mentioned by the children.

Now that we were aware that the settings of stories were important, we turned to *Johnny Crow's Garden*, which we explored as a contrasting area. The illustrations were projected on a large screen and, using their skills of examining and interpreting visual details, the children were able to see that it was a *locus amoenus* and a reflection of the character of the good-natured host. In fact, the *locus amoenus* was introduced, not as something to be learned or memorized, but as an interesting pair of words which, I told them, I often used in my teaching at the university. (They had visited my university classes and were aware that I was an English professor.) In further discussions, the children discovered and commented on how Johnny Crow's personality and his garden had a beneficial effect on his guests. Finally, we compared the two gardens, Johnny's and Mr. McGregor's. We noticed, for example, that Johnny's garden portal bore a welcome sign and that Mr. McGregor's did not; that Johnny provided for his guests and that Mr. McGregor tried to capture an interloper; and that a dinner party marked the culmination of the crow's entertainments, whereas eating nearly proved the undoing of Peter, who ran the danger of becoming a pie himself.

At last, as we moved slowly toward Edmonton's long delayed but anxiously awaited spring, we were ready to tackle our most ambitious and penultimate project of the school year: the reading and discussing of Frances Hodgson Burnett's The Secret Garden. I say ambitious because the book is long — nearly three hundred pages; complex — there are at least ten significant characters; and (in most editions) virtually unillustrated — the children would have to depend on the words alone for the understanding of what was going on. The study of The Secret Garden marked the culmination of the program, as it drew on virtually all of the skills developed during the year.

Our analytical focus was directed to the changing state of the garden as an indicator of the developing characters of Mary Lennox and Colin Craven. After reading the early chapters and discussing Mary's contrary nature, we looked at her Indian hibiscus garden and the nursery rhyme, seeing how both reflected Mary's own nature. We then noticed how different from Johnny Crow and his garden Mary and hers were. At important points in the novel, the children were encouraged to relate Mary's and later Colin's character growth to the changes in the secret garden. In addition, both Mary and Colin were discussed in relation to such lonely characters as Crow Boy and Jacob Two-Two, both examined earlier in the year.

In order that they could more clearly see the changes occurring in Mary, Colin and Mr. Craven, each child kept a line graph on which he indicated, after each chapter, whether he felt each character to be more or less happy. This was not the first graph the class had used. A month earlier, while reading Jacob Two-Two Meets the Hooded Fang, I had constructed a large graph which I had placed on the wall. After graphing myself the unhappiness or happiness of the hero in the first three chapters, I invited the class to suggest whether or not they felt I should move the line up or down after each significant event. They had enjoyed the activity and now, given their own graphs for *The Secret Garden*, they responded eagerly. The experiment progressed well. Of course, some of the children handled the graphs with greater ease than others, and each of the graphs was different. Indeed, uniformity was not the goal. However, explanation of individual decisions was encouraged.*

Stott's description of a deep study with children shows what it is possible to grow towards. But it also emphasizes what I have been saying over and over again: that it is not enough to know our children well and to know the books well; we must also know something of the way books relate to each other. Quite clearly, most adults can never know enough about the books to be able to deal with them as Stott did. That is why the professional teacher and librarian, whose responsibility it is to know the books well and who specializes in the teaching of literature to children, are necessary and always will be.

I have suggested that adults ask themselves all these seven questions. But questions One to Three also guide the adult's book-talk with children. They are a blueprint for critical discussion with readers of any age and experience.

    In Chapter seventeen I give an example of those questions being answered as I prepared myself to introduce *Slake's Limbo* by Felice Holman to young readers. Before this, however, we need to remind ourselves what is involved in an intelligent appreciation of a literary work from a traditional and secure point of view.

*Jon Stott, "Criticism and the Teaching of Stories to Children," *Signal* 32, May 1980, pp. 81-92.

XVI

Taking Pleasure: An Adult Reads

Anybody who can perform the act of reading can find a work of literature to enjoy. One of the great glories of books is that there are plenty to suit everybody, no matter what our taste, our mood, our intellectual ability, age, living experience. Anybody who can read and talk can find something to say about what has been read, and so is able to share the pleasure, the puzzles, the connections found in a book.

For adults dealing with children and their reading in a professional and teaching role, however, that hit-or-miss, easy-going way of reading is not enough. We need to know more about literature; how it is made, how to read it thoughtfully, how to take from a book everything it has to offer. We need to be more conscious than most people, most non-professional readers are, just as any professional is expected to be more knowledgeable and more skilled than non-professionals in any walk of life. If we are not, we cannot properly help children become thoughtful readers themselves.

Many people have written on this subject, some at inordinate length. Lord David Cecil, who spent his life as a reader and teacher of literature, managed to say the important things in a few uncomplicated pages.

THE APPRECIATION OF LITERATURE
by Lord David Cecil

Up to a year or two ago, I was for forty years a don at Oxford. It was an agreeable life. Day after day I would sit in my room in college, teaching young people to enjoy themselves. All dons don't do this — historians needn't, or philosophers. But I taught

English literature, and that is different. There are many books published in the world and of many kinds, but one category stands apart: books that come under the heading of literature. This means books not written for any ulterior purpose but simply to give the reader a satisfying experience, such as he would have from a piece of music or a beautiful picture; their aim is to delight. Of course, the greatest art does much more. Shakespeare, Tolstoy, Wordsworth, Dante give us wisdom and spiritual vision. But delight is the means. Unless we enjoy their writings, we shall not perceive the vision and the wisdom. Therefore it follows that the first aim of a reader is to be delighted. To do this fully he must develop his faculty of appreciation. That is what I tried to help the young people to do, in my room at Oxford. Appreciation is not a simple process: a lot of professional critics have never learnt how to do it. They seem to take a positive pleasure in telling you that they do not enjoy things. They explain that they think Dickens much overrated, or that they can't stand Charles Lamb — as if not to enjoy what has pleased Tolstoy and Virginia Woolf was something to be proud of. As a matter of fact, to achieve a wide appreciation does need self-training.

First of all, it needs the right approach: one must realize what a work of literary art is; and in particular that it is the result of two impulses. For one thing, it is the record of a personal vision. For example, on a May evening in 1819, Keats sat in a garden in Hampstead and listened to the song of a nightingale. He listened with rapture, and all the more because it was a poignant moment in his life. He had lately been watching his brother, of whom he was very fond, die of consumption. Keats contrasted the grim facts of reality, as he had just seen them, with the sense of bliss stirred in him by the song of the nightingale. A flood of feeling welled up in him — about life and death and beauty and suffering and transitoriness and the yearning of his unsatisfied soul for a happiness not to be found on earth — which poured out in "Ode to a Nightingale." Keats wanted to tell us about his feelings. But this was not the only motive for his writing the poem. People don't become painters just because there is one particular subject they want to paint: they also enjoy constructing a pleasing object in line and color. It is the same with poets. If Keats had just wanted to say what he felt, he could have done it in prose. But he wanted to construct a pleasing object in word and rhythmic verse. It is the blend of the two impulses, the impulse to record the personal vision and the impulse to construct an object in verse, which produced the unique phenomenon called "Ode to a Nightingale."

The aim of the reader is to perceive such phenomena and respond to them. This does mean accepting, for the time being, the kind of vision and the kind of form. I stress this again because people often reject one or the other or both. I've heard people say they did not admire Thomas Hardy's novels because they were gloomy. They cannot be forced to like them: but it's no good blaming them for being gloomy. Hardy had a tragic vision of life and that indeed is what the novels portray. People should never start with strong preconceived ideas about what the work ought to be like. Any writer, if he is any good, has something of his own to say. That is his vision; and the new vision nearly always means a slight modification of form. We should try to accept both.

We must also be sure that we understand the language in which the work is composed. I don't mean just the words: but language as a metaphor for its whole mode of expression. Three things are entailed here.

First, there is the convention in which it is written. All literature is written in some convention; and failure to realize this has led very clever people to say very foolish things. Voltaire was one of the cleverest men who ever lived, but he had been brought up on the French classical tragedy of Racine and Corneille: formal, restrained, regular. That was his idea of tragedy. He came to England and went to see *Hamlet*. He thought it appalling: a crude barbaric mixture of verse and prose, poetry and realism, crammed with ghosts, corpses, maniacs — all very unlike Racine. But we must not be too scornful of foreign Voltaire. A little later Hazlitt, one of our best critics, but who was brought up on Shakespeare, read Racine. He didn't react quite as strongly as Voltaire, but he thought it poor stuff: artificial, pedantic, dull. He hadn't accepted its convention. As a matter of fact, Shakespeare and Racine were both great writers and also not as unlike as all that: they were both masters of passionate, noble tragedy, but expressed in different conventions, both of which the reader should learn to accept.

I once failed to do this myself with disastrous results. When I was twenty-one I went to see my first Chekhov play — *The*

Cherry Orchard, it may have been. I thought the way the characters talked unreal. People didn't seem to reply to each other. One might say, "How noisy the birds are," and another would reply: "I've not had a good education, though it was in Moscow." Also they were strangely outspoken, and might say to each other: "Why do you bore me so much?" I thought it all very unreal. I was not used to the convention by which Chekhov, in order to reveal what was in the minds of his characters, would make them utter it straight out. If they were thinking about being educated in Moscow, they said so; and if they were bored, they told each other so. Of course, it may have been that in Chekhov's world people did talk like this. But they don't do so in other Russian books. I think it is his convention. In fact, as he had extraordinary insight into human nature, this convention makes him convey the reality of the independent lives and thoughts of his different people about what is happening to them much better than he could have without it. Now I say categorically that the most realistic plays I've ever read or seen are the plays of Chekhov.

The second language to be learnt is the language of period. This applies less to modern than to older works. A past period is like a foreign country. It is a region inhabited by human beings of like passions to our own, but with different customs and traditions. If we don't understand these customs and traditions we shall misunderstand books of that particular period. Let me take an instance from Shakespeare's *Measure for Measure*. In this play Isabella, the heroine, refuses Angelo's dishonorable proposal to her though it would save Claudio her brother's life if she yielded; and she does this in spite of the fact that Claudio beseeches her to yield. For her refusal, Isabella has received a great deal of blame from subsequent critics, who call her a hard-hearted prude. In fact, to blame her is to show a fatal ignorance of the beliefs of Shakespeare's age, according to which if she had agreed, she would have committed a mortal sin and been in danger of hell. And Claudio would have been too, for urging her to yield. She cannot therefore be blamed much for refusing.

Finally, one must learn what I would call the language of the author's personality and temperament. This is a more complex task. Every book is the expression of a man or a woman and to approach the book properly one must adapt oneself to his viewpoint. Each author has his private window on reality, different from other men's windows. Different things are visible from it, and the same things are seen in a different proportion and different perspective. One must try, while reading, to look at every book from that author's particular window and see life from his viewpoint. Now this third language is much the hardest to learn, for each of us has his own viewpoint and can't divest himself of it entirely. It is hard for a militant atheist to appreciate a religious book, for a puritan type to like Tom Jones. This is a particular difficulty in judging contemporary work. Hazlitt said, very truly, that all living authors are our friends or our foes. I remember, when I was young, that progressive pacific kinds of people could not admire Kipling because he represented the militant imperialism which they disliked. At the same time, militant imperialist kinds of people couldn't admire Shaw, who, they thought, was a dangerous socialist revolutionary. Both were wrong: Kipling and Shaw are both writers of genius. Now it is easy to realize this because they no longer stand for living controversies: Kipling's brand of imperialism and Shaw's brand of revolutionary socialism are both things of the past. What remains is their genius; and we respond to that freely.

Of course, human imperfection will always limit our powers of appreciation. I've never been able fully to enjoy what I am told is the best novel written in my lifetime: James Joyce's *Ulysses*. I recognize Joyce's genius, and that there are bright flashes of it in *Ulysses*. But, in the main, I find it often boring and sometimes repellent. But I also realize that this is partly because it is so far from my individual taste in subject and style that I have not been able to learn its language. On the other hand, Jane Austen's view of life and type of art are so naturally sympathetic to me that it is possible — though I don't think it is probable — that I overrate her. Yet the fact that one will never be perfectly good is no reason for not trying to be as good as one can be; and, in the same way, the fact that one will never achieve a perfectly just and comprehensive taste is no reason for not trying to refine and broaden one's taste as much as one can. Certainly, now I am sixty-eight years old I do enjoy a lot of books that I didn't enjoy at eighteen. Then I had a romantic taste in poetry; I thought it ought to be dreamy and rapturous and inspiring; and I found it extraordinary when somebody said to me that he liked Pope's poetry as much as Keats's. Now I delight in Pope; but I still like Keats as much as ever. Nor does this broadening of taste make it undiscriminating. On the contrary, it grows more impartial but also more discriminating: because, having adapted the mind to the convention, to the period, to the personality, one is much more able to take the work on its own terms and thus perceive more clearly when it fails. One gets less partisan, one is able to see faults even in one's favorites. I delight in Jane Austen, largely because I think her stories so true to life. But for this very reason I notice all the more when I think they are not. I find the end of *Mansfield Park* unconvincing. There, if you remember, Henry Crawford, having been refused by the heroine Fanny, goes off and elopes with an old flame, Mrs. Rushworth. For me the reason for this is clear: Jane Austen wants to get him out of the way so that Fanny can marry the hero Edmund. Also she wants to emphasize that Henry really was a very undesirable type. All the same, I think the incident improbable because he has been represented up till then as a cold, careful character. Why then should he involve himself with a woman he was already tired of? It is not made clear. Perhaps Jane Austen was aware of this, for having stated the fact of the elopement briefly, she says airily: "Let other pens dwell on guilt and misery, I quit such odious subjects as soon as I can." One may sympathize with her in this. All the same, she was mistaken. She needed to dwell a little on the "odious subject" if she was to make her story convincing.

To develop appreciation means that one notes faults as well as merits. Yet the gain in pleasure is greater than the loss. For to train one's taste is to increase one's capacity for enjoyment: it enables one to enter into such a variety of experience. That is the great gift literature can give one. In real life, experience is limited. The same person cannot be both a man and a woman, a saint and a sinner, a stay-at-home and an explorer, an ancient Roman and a modern Russian. But books can teach us all to be all those things in imagination. The Lady of Shalott sat in her tower watching the diverse pageant of human life pass before her in a mirror. The reader is like her: he sits watching the diverse pageant of human thought and human feeling passing across the gleaming mirror of literature. And like the Lady of Shalott's, it is a magic mirror, for it turns all it reflects into matter for delight. It is not so in reality. Reality is often very much lacking in delight. So is the reality described in books.

Let me mention three favorites: *War and Peace, The Mayor of Casterbridge* by Thomas Hardy and *Emma*. None of them represents life at its most attractive. The battles in *War and Peace* are the last things I would like to be present at. It would be sad to live in Hardy's Casterbridge. Emma's home is pleasanter; but it is a little dull. Yet I enjoy reading about all three. In them, by the magic power of art, lead and mud have been turned into gold; horror, gloom, dullness, because they have been made part of the vision of a great writer and transfigured by his art, are changed into matter for delight. And it is a delight that lasts. I am now an elderly retired person, and as such I look back over the years and ask myself what satisfactions have proved the most lasting. Many have not lasted. I am too old any longer to play games or dance; my social life is restricted; and I cannot, as I used, take much interest in the future of the world, for I shan't live long enough to see what is going to happen in it. But the satisfaction given by reading is unimpaired. Prose and poetry, novels and plays, essays and biographies — I enjoy them all as much as ever. The world round me may have grown dimmer with the passing of the years, but not the world reflected in the magic mirror of literature. That is still as fresh and vivid and fascinating and enthralling as it was when I was fifteen years old.*

In crudely schematic terms, David Cecil is suggesting we ask ourselves a few simple questions about any work of literature as we read it and afterwards.

1. What kind of work is this?
2. What does its author want me to accept and give myself up to as part of his vision and the work he has created?
3. What convention does the work employ?
4. What historical period does the work belong to; when and where was it written?
5. What do we know of the author's personality and temperament that might help us understand the work?
6. What is there about myself as a person and as a reader that gets in the way of the work, and of my enjoyment and under-

*Lord David Cecil, "The Appreciation of Literature," *The Listener*, December 9, 1971, pp. 797 ff.

standing of it, or that causes me to attach so much (too much?) importance to it?

7. What are the work's weaknesses and strengths, as far as I can discover them?

These are questions that add to and reinforce those I suggested we ask of our reading in the previous chapter.

Now we must look at an example of a reading experience in order to see how those questions get answered so that we can observe the process in action.

XVII
Enjoying *Slake's Limbo*

Slake's Limbo by Felice Holman was first published by Charles Scribner in 1974 and was selected as an American Library Association Notable Book for that year. The paperback appeared from Dell in 1977 and a British hardcover edition from Macmillan in 1980. A review by Mary M. Burns in *The Horn Book Magazine* provides us with a useful summary of the novel's plot:

> "[S]mall, nearsighted, dreaming, bruised, an outlander in the city of his birth," thirteen-year-old Aremis Slake fled one day to the only refuge he knew — the New York subway system. He was to remain there for one hundred and twenty-one days, an urban Robinson Crusoe, venturing forth from his hiding hole in the walls beneath the Commodore Hotel at Grand Central Station to retrieve salvageable materials from the jettisoned impedimenta of restless travelers. As his confidence grows, he begins to make a success of his scavenging, becoming an underground entrepreneur and an explorer of the world beneath the streets. The economically told chronicle of Slake's adventures is more than a survival saga; it is also an eloquent study of poverty, of fear, and finally of hope — as circumstances converge to force Slake from his temporary limbo. Ill with pneumonia, he is rescued by a subway trainman and taken to Bellevue Hospital. As he recovers, he overhears a well-intentioned social worker murmuring soothingly about a juvenile facility, and contrives an escape. He heads back to the subway but, at the last moment, reverses direction. "Slake did not know exactly where he was going, but the general direction was up." Stark, carefully-wrought, the narrative contrasts sharply with the comic tone of the author's recent *Escape of the Giant Hogstalk*, indicating a remarkably versatile talent.*

*Mary M. Burns, in "Early Spring Booklist." *The Horn Book Magazine*, April 1975, pp. 149-150.

One important element is missed from this notice: the chapters titled "On Another Track," interwoven, so to speak, with Slake's story, in which we are told about Willis Joe Whinny, the motor-man who drives the subway train that eventually almost kills Slake, but who instead rescues him from his underground life. Willis Joe, like Slake, is a would-be escaper. His dream is to leave the USA, in favor of sheep farming in Australia.

I first came across *Slake's Limbo* when I was visiting the University of Iowa and a copy was put into my hands by Professor Robert Carlsen, whose guest I was at the Faculty of Education. The copy was grubby from use, a paperback with a photographically realistic full-color painting on its cover of an early teenage boy slumped in what looked to me like a corner of a very dirty back alley, a can of Coke in his hand. I would not have given the book a second glance had I seen it lying about somewhere. But Bob Carlsen is a friend whose knowledge of books for young people I respect and trust, and *Slake's Limbo*, he said, as he gave me the copy, was a book I had to know. I read it in one sitting as soon as I got home. Proof again of the fact that all of us — children and adults — are most influenced in choosing what we read by recommendations made by our friends.

Apart from a dislike of its grubby state, two things occurred to me as I settled down to read the novel. The first was that the American paperback cover was very well chosen to attract the sort of reluctant eleven-to-fifteen-year-old readers I had often faced during my career as a teacher-librarian. The second was that the book was very short (the British hardback is only 119 pages), which pleased me because I am a slow reader and jealous of my reading time; I was not, to be honest, expecting to enjoy the novel and was reading it as a duty, having promised Bob that I would.

I have learned not to read blurbs, but *Slake* has a kind of introductory paragraph that acts like a blurb yet is clearly meant as part of the text:

> Aremis Slake, at the age of thirteen, took his fear and misfortune and hid them underground. The thing is, he had to go with them.

This struck me, in my prejudiced, dutiful mood, as somewhat

high-flown, even as a little precious. A thirteen-year-old hiding his
fear underground . . . of course he had to go with it. Tautology
in two sentences. I was not doing too well. I was, I suspected, in
for yet another of those numerously produced fantasies in which
a pubescent child gets involved with underworld beings that are
actually surrogates for Freudian or Jungian types, substandard versions of Le Guin's *The Wizard of Earthsea*, or peritonitic spin-
offs from the detritus of ill-digested Tolkien.

I surmise, as I dutifully begin, that *Slake* will start in the
hard-edged reality of modern urban life before sliding ineluctably
into the darkling land of Elsewhere. The first paragraph was
therefore expected:

> The thing that happened, when finally it happened, was so
> perfectly logical that it should not really be considered sur-
> prising. Because the fact is that even earlier in life Aremis Slake
> had often escaped into the subway when things got rough above
> ground. He kept a subway token in his pocket for just that
> emergency, and the emergencies kept occurring due to a joining
> of hostile circumstances.

Professor Carlsen, I decided, had gone off his head. This style
was not only Latinate it was also self-consciously high-flown —
the rhythm of that repeated opening phrase, "The thing that
happened, when finally it happened . . ." so carefully judged to
sound distanced, controlled, semi-lyrical. Perfectly formed, "the
emergencies kept occurring due to a joining of hostile circumstances. . . ." Disaffected and literally unliterary pubescent readers were expected to be hooked by this? Not the ones I knew.
But, no no — I must resist that teacherly instinct to read everything on behalf of the children. First, the important thing is to
sum up a book as for oneself, not for anyone else.

The second paragraph came down to earth stylistically. But
of its four sentences, the third was so determined to present a
grammatically structured metaphor for its meaning that it
dazzled my eye, never mind my already unsympathetic brain:

> But he was wiry and wily, too, and he could often out-run,
> tack, back-track, double-back, and finally dodge unseen into the
> subway, hiding, if possible, in some nook of the station to save

the fare, or riding, if necessary, till things cooled off and the
world above became habitable again.

All those commas, all those alliterative processions of sometimes
half-rhymed words: "wiry and wily," "out-run, tack, back-track,
double-back," "unseen into the subway . . . possible, in some
nook of the station, to save . . ." Too much of this would be
torture. Would I get through to the end?

One thing kept me reading. Slake. Even by the end of the
first uncomfortable page he was present, a person I could see (I
had taught a number of him) standing in front of me, so to
speak. Small, lithe, myopic, shy, uncommunicative, vulnerable.
And a dreamer. I hated, though, and still do, that sentence,
"Slake dreamed and walked a dreamer." More of that fanciful,
romanticizing style, I thought. I do have to add, however, that
this rapid character drawing was a touch spoiled by the bathos
— the other side of the high-flying style — of Slake being such a
dreamer that he bumps into lampposts. Street boys like Slake
— wily, a dodger used to running away — do not, even when they
are myopic and dreamers, allow themselves to bump into lampposts. Indeed, thinking back over the first page, as I turned to
page two, Slake seemed perhaps a shade too afflicted, an anti-
hero with everything loaded against him.

The character-making goes on for a couple of pages till we
come to a line gap. I am by now waiting for the first hint that
the expected fantasy-time has arrived. I am beginning to think I
will give up when it does. But no, we are drawn by a flashback
into Slake's home. Holman has decided we must see Slake's
background, and it is as bleak and oppressive as one supposed it
must be. We meet Slake's only friend, the silent, ever-smiling,
"mystical" Joseph, later to learn he has been killed by a truck.
Slake is, as he has to be for the purposes of the story, alone — for
who, after all, could stay with his fear below ground for (what
is it?) one hundred and twenty-one days without someone, a
relative or friend, doing something about finding him?

Another line gap. The new section opens: "So the day of
the sweater — the end of the beginning." Another of those
near-cliché phrases. But we must be nearing the first events of
the main plot. Slake is chased into the subway and comes out

again into Central Park, New York City. And here I think I have found it at last: that fantasy:

> At the sight of the park, something came back to Slake. It was the recurrence of an old fantasy that *this year the leaves would stay on the trees.*

The italics are Holman's. I am reading as rapidly as I ever read now, not in order to find out what will happen next, but to reach the point where my prejudices will be confirmed by Slake's entrance into his Never-never Land. Expectations run high — and are confounded. For Slake is disturbed in his daydream by shouts from his pursuers who have found him again; but no, it is the park attendant. Slake runs frantically to the safety of the subway once more. And now, with the end of chapter one, I really am reading to see what will happen next, for the plot has not fulfilled my doubts.

I go with Slake into the tunnel, find with him his hide-out and learn, what he could not know, how that cavernous room came into being. The possibility of it is entertaining and, more importantly, absorbing.

Chapter two ends. I turn over to find, set in a different typeface, the first of the interwoven chapters about Willis Joe: "On Another Track." What's this? At first I am irritated by this interruption of my plot-based excitement, forgetting that only a few moments ago I was all ready to give up reading because the book was not going to be to my taste. And then, another side of me is engaged. I have a liking for novels which use techniques for disturbing the usual steady flow of sequential narrative with perhaps a flashback or two, and a balance between narrative commentary and dialogue. *Slake* has been conventional, ordinary in this regard so far; now, suddenly, I am presented with a change of typeface; what appears to be another story; a new, adult, character; and a time-scale in relation to Slake's story that I find it at first a little difficult to decide about. (Is it a parallel time with Slake's or is it out of gear with him?) What I soon know is that I like this extra dimension, this second thread of plot so neatly designed to give relief from Slake and also to highlight his adventure. In what I had come to think of as an insignificant little book with its direct and simple story, this is an unexpected find. I am now completely absorbed, keen to follow not just the events of the story but the author's handling of them too. Form and content are meshing unexpectedly.

So I read on, with increasing interest and enjoyment, and, let it be said, admiration too. Space prevents my describing the whole reading in detail; nor is it necessary that I should, for what I intend is to give a sample of how that first blueprint question, "What happened to me as I read this book?" is being answered through the story of my reading — which I will use as the raw material for a critical exploration of what this book is and means; how best to present it to children; and what kind of talk children can engage in with an adult as they try to sort out their own reading of the same book.

The answers to the second question, "Which features of the book caused my responses?" are already becoming clear: what it was in me that was engaged, provoked, stimulated; what it was in the book that held my attention. The cover picture of the paperback edition I was reading — the book-as-object — raised certain expectations about the readership, and the nature of the text I would encounter. Coupled of course with the things Bob Carlsen had said to me: that this was a book he admired and that "worked" extremely well with many teenagers he knew; that it was one of those books we all are always looking for that rivets the attention of, and gives pleasure to, non-literary, reluctant readers as well as to literary readers. The first words I read raised expectations about the kind of story I was tackling, expectations which proved unfounded and were reformed by the end of the third chapter. These were ideas brought into play by my own personal prejudices resulting from my reading history — prejudices against a certain kind of fantasy. The book's linguistic style made me uneasy and I kept trying to pinpoint the reason. Was it the way the author used words and the tone of voice created by that Latinate, urbane style? Or was it a different attitude to language between the English and the Americans? (The English tend to like something more spare, less decorated, in their modern novels, whereas the Americans often go in for the more colorful and verbose.)

Set against all this was the character of Slake himself, drawn in great detail and, for me, vividly present and believable, if extreme in his oppressed and victimized nature. This, at first, was the feature of the novel that kept me going: a liking for the protagonist. Later, with the entrance of Willis Joe, and the author's treatment of that thread of the story, other attractions made themselves clear. I began to live in the alternative world of the book itself, questioning less, criticizing less, and believing more.

So I could go on, unraveling the causes of my responses. But essentially what happened to me was that I began to read the book the author had made, not the one I was trying at first to turn it into. I began to discover, in other words, the answers to the third question, "What does this book ask of its readers if they are to enjoy what it offers and discover its potentialities?"

Standing back after my first reading to contemplate my experience I began to see that one of the important things about *Slake's Limbo* is that it succeeds in creating vividly the life Slake made for himself below ground. His limbo is from the first totally convincing to me because Holman builds it up through precise, realistically accurate details. She works through the minutiae of Slake's life. In this sense the book resembles that masterpiece, *One Day in the Life of Ivan Denisovitch*, Solzhenitsyn's novel about one good day in the life of one of Stalin's victims living out a wretched existence in a Siberian prison camp. In both stories it is through a steady build-up of concrete detail and a concentration on the ordinary pleasures and difficulties of life that the book's world is made convincing. No great dramas, no pyrotechnics in action or thought. But an account of eating and sleeping, the making of a home against the odds, the finding of pleasure where none seemed possible, human initiative, human invention, human intelligence applied to the creation of happiness. For beneath the ground, shut in his dark cave, Slake discovers for the first time how he could make a life for himself, instead of always living a life forced on him by other people. "It might be said of Slake," Holman writes at the end, "that he had spent all of his life on the underside of stones. For the first time now he became sharply aware that he was walking *on*, not under." Just as Ivan finds that by taking pleasure in an extra piece of food, in the laying of bricks as his day's work, and in finding and managing to keep a broken and discarded hacksaw blade he makes survival possible and beats Stalin and his jailors at their own game.

That style, which was at first so annoying to me, settles down by chapter three — or I had grown used to it? — and begins to show its strength. Holman uses it because it refuses to allow the reader to think as Slake, in the way a first-person narrative would have encouraged. And because it refuses to express itself in the kind of language we have to assume would be natural to Slake himself — slangy, staccato, flip, street-wise — we are forced into the position of *observing* him rather than feeling at one with him. Holman wants us to think about Slake and his predicament, rather than to fight it out with him. We are to be spectators not participants. So the narrator's style has to be articulate, cultivated, correct, steady. It can, also therefore, tell us things about Slake that Slake could never tell us about himself, either because he cannot know them or could never find words to express them.

In this respect *Slake's Limbo* is different from most of the novels written for and about people of Slake's age and background, from *Catcher in the Rye* to the stories like those by Zindel and S. E. Hinton, which usually ask us to go inside the character, and are often written in the first person. When *Slake's Limbo* first appeared in 1974 the rap-talk narrative style was at a fashionable high point, which made *Slake* seem all the more refreshing, and may even account for some of its critical and popular success. For it is not, I think, quite as important a book as its reception suggested. But more of that in a moment.

"On Another Track" also helped lift *Slake* out of the ordinary. Few short novels which appear on booklists for children and young adults are even modestly interesting from the technical point of view. Zindel's surface devices (handwritten letters, facsimile invitation cards, newspaper clippings, and so on) to be found in *My Darling, My Hamburger*, for example, are entertaining and often remarked upon. But they remain surface devices. They are not made to reverberate with any deeper layers of the story or to mesh with other technically different ways of telling the story. In other words, writers for children and young adults are far too limited in their use of the possibilities that lie in the book-as-object, and the narrative techniques frequently employed in mainstream, adult literature in order to present a more multi-layered and multi-faceted story world. Whereas, however modestly, Willis Joe's other track gives *Slake* a density and a greater subtlety, and therefore an irony of viewpoint that enhances it as a story and gives it a greater importance in the context of books for young people than it would otherwise have possessed.

By thus pinning down what the book is and how it works I gradually sharpen my understanding, and discover those features I most want children to heed. Even taken only this far we can already see that there is plenty in *Slake's Limbo* that makes it worth my time and the young readers' time. So the answers to question four are easy to list. A short novel that will interest a wide range of readers (wide-ranging in literary skill and experience), the book brings together numerous ideas that preoccupy pubescent children — ideas about:

> personal identity;
> what "home" means;
> oppression;
> who you "belong" to and who "belongs" to you;
> the nature of courage and "facing up to life";
> the mechanics and morality of survival in a modern city
> (Is theft ever justifiable? What rights have the dispossessed? What is "the law"? etc.);
> the nature of human dignity and what you actually need to
> stay alive and build a life that offers more than bare
> existence.

These and other ideas are explored through a clearly-drawn central character with whom it is easy to sympathize, and a narrative pattern made interesting by two main features: the way it makes the reader stand back and observe the protagonist; and the way it uses a parallel story about Willis Joe to counterpoint the one about Slake, till the two are brought together to effect a satisfying resolution to Slake's underground life and his self-imposed "limbo."

Over and above all this, and the book's most subtle feature (one not yet remarked on here and which would be the most difficult to help children come to grips with) is the novel's metaphoric nature. Slake, his life in the tunnel and around the subway, and Willis Joe's parallel life are all metaphors for the life going on above ground. Such obvious meanings as Slake being like a rat in a maze — a symbol of life in a modern city; or of tunnels with caverns inside them being surrogates for the womb — and thus Slake's return to that state; or his rebirth through the intervention of the penis-father, Willis Joe — these are too crude. But they do point us in the right direction and set us off on a discussion of fiction as a symbolic structure that is to life what metaphors are to reality; and about the modernist idea — found in the work of the structuralist and phenomenological critics — that the fiction should always be seen to be a fiction, that we should be kept aware of the story as marks made with ink on paper, something which the change in the typeface for the setting of the "On Another Track" chapters hints at in *Slake*. The linguistic style too is frequently metaphoric, one of the reasons for my feeling that it was overly-decorated when I began reading. We would though, as I said, find it hard and perhaps not useful to get as far as this kind of discussion with most pubescent readers; and if we did we should need to find a language in which to talk about such ideas that would be nearer to their own.

All-in-all, then, plenty to attend to, plenty to enjoy, plenty to share. So now, question five: How best to mediate the book to children? *Slake's Limbo* reads aloud well and is short enough, and also appropriately arranged in chapters of a suitable length to manage with eleven-to-fourteen-year-olds in a week of daily readings lasting about thirty minutes each. Because it is so "visually" told — Slake and his life are easy to picture — it could also be read aloud without the need for everyone to have a copy to follow. And its episodic plot, without the kind of mystery climax that has to be led up to without interruption (this is not an action-centered, but a contemplative and feeling-centered novel) means that the gaps between readings won't spoil the effect. Indeed they might for some readers be beneficial, allowing opportunity for talk about Slake and what is happening to him, and the nature of his story, that will actually increase understanding and pleasure as the readings progress. There would also be time, for those who want to, to find out about the New York subway system and how it works, background information that will add interest for some reader-listeners.

Slake's Limbo is as near perfect a novel as one can hope to find for this sort of group-experienced close reading. But if for some reason I were to decide not to bring it before children in this way, preferring them to read it for themselves and by their own choice, then I would introduce it during one of my "Have you read this?" sessions, when I would do two things. First, say very briefly that this is a story about a thirteen-year-old boy who lives in New York and is so often the victim of street bullies that he hides in the subway, where he manages to make a home for himself and live for one-hundred-and-twenty-one days on his own. I would deliberately avoid raising expectations that this is going to be an exciting action-packed read, but rather that the real interest is in Slake himself and the way we are shown in great detail how he sets about feeding and looking after himself without anyone to help him and while having to keep his home hidden.

The second thing I would do is read the first two chapters, as a kind of appetizer, though in fact my secret purpose would be to help familiarize everybody with the book's linguistic style and approach, because my judgment is that many children would be likely to find this a barrier and might therefore give up reading before the book has had a chance to convert them into the kind of reader it looks for.

As always when expecting a fairly enthusiastic response I would have ready at least six copies of the paperback edition if possible to hand out immediately to those who want them. Everything we know about reading tells us that the connection between a desire to read a particular book and its immediate availability is important. The desire soon dies away and the book is forgotten if copies are not handy.

Question five. *Slake's Limbo* has an interesting authorial back-ground. Felice Holman tells the story of its writing in an article, "*Slake's Limbo*: In Which a Book Switches Authors."* I would certainly want to retell that story to young readers, in abbreviated form, if the book excited them. I might also use some informa-tion from it to help raise interest if I were simply recommending the book — such as the fact that Holman actually explored the subway tunnels and found a real cavern like the one in the book, and learned to drive a subway train in order to get Willis Joe's details right. There are also biographical entries in *Something About the Author* (Gale) and *Twentieth Century Children's Writers* (St. Martin's, U.S.A./Macmillan, U.K.) which will pro-vide information for those who want to follow up the author's background. Obviously I would have to hand a large scale map of the New York subway system ready to show children who did not know about it, and would also have dug out information references to which readers can be directed who want to know more about the setting.

My last blueprint question asks about the literary context. *Slake's Limbo* belongs to a large category of fiction that deals in exile, whether enforced or self-sought. It points the way to *One Day in the Life of Ivan Denisovitch* by Alexander Solzhenitsyn, to my mind one of the modern classics. But that is three or four years ahead for even *Slake's* most enthusiastic readers. Yet we can hope that some of the more experienced children, to whom we are likely to offer *Slake's Limbo*, will have read or be ready for *Robinson Crusoe*. Mary Burns makes the connection between the two novels in her review, and Holman herself makes it in her article. Defoe's story is of course much more testing of a reader's stamina and willingness to come to grips with what many chil-dren will think of as an "old-fashioned" style of writing; but if *Slake* leads to them at least trying *Robinson* then much progress has been made. At the same level of difficulty as *Slake*, and standing just to one side of it — and perhaps coming a little

*Felice Holman, "*Slake's Limbo*: In Which a Book Switches Authors," *The Horn Book Magazine*, October 1976, pp. 479-485.

earlier in reading progress — is Betsy Byars's *The Eighteenth Emergency*, the connection being, of course, that both stories deal in oppression and fear, and both treat (though in different ways) the metaphoric value of fiction by incorporating it into the fabric of the story — in *Slake*, through its use of images (the tunnel, etc.) and in *The Eighteenth Emergency* through its use of Ezzie's "emergencies" and Mouse's fantasizing around them.

John Rowe Townsend's *Trouble in the Jungle* connects with the exile and home-making themes, but in this case they are handled socially; the story involves a group of children who, deserted by their parents, are forced out of their family home and set up an alternative and secret home in a disused building. Townsend's story suits the same age-and-reading range as *Slake*, as does Armstrong Sperry's *Call It Courage*, now some years old but still to my mind an attractive and alive book, as short as *Slake* and equally good to read aloud in a few serial sessions. Here the connecting themes are courage and cowardice and what these are; facing your self; survival on your own in hostile surroundings — this time on a taboo island used by cannibals. Sperry's story also performs the useful function of universalizing these ideas by placing them in a time and place and culture quite different from a modern city.

Thus we could continue sorting out *Slake's* literary pedigree, and preparing for the answer to that question that signals the success of every book: Have you another book like it that I could read?

I should emphasize again that this attempt to demonstrate my blueprint in action is not an exhaustive study of *Slake's Limbo*, but rather *Slake's Limbo* has been used simply to indicate how I would set about answering my own questions. And in sum I would have to decide as a result of the answers that, though modest in its achievements, *Slake's Limbo* is certainly worth attention, and is one of those books which are so valuable in part because they acquire fairly easily for themselves, and give pleasure to, a wide spectrum of readers, providing a reading experience rich enough and varied enough for most children to find something they can and want to share.

Bibliography

Briggs, Katherine M., ed. *A Dictionary of British Folk-Tales in the English Language*. 4 vols. London: Routledge and Kegan Paul, 1970-71/ Bloomington, Ind.: Indiana University Press.

Britton, James. *Language and Learning*. London: Allen Lane, 1970/ Miami: University of Miami Press, 1970.

Cecil, Lord David. "The Appreciation of Literature," *The Listener*, December 9, 1971.

Chambers, Aidan. "Letter from England: Having Fun Feeling Famous," *The Horn Book Magazine*, April 1982.

Chambers, Aidan. "The Reader in the Book," *The Signal Approach to Children's Books*. Nancy Chambers, ed. London: Kestrel, 1980/ Metuchen, N. J.: Scarecrow Press, 1981.

Commire, Anne, ed. *Something About the Author: Facts and Pictures About Contemporary Authors and Illustrators of Books for Young People*. vols. 1-26. Detroit, Mich.: 1971-1982.

Cook, Elizabeth. *The Ordinary and the Fabulous*. 2nd ed. Cambridge: Cambridge University Press, 1975.

Daiches, David. *Critical Approaches to Literature*. Englewood Cliffs, N. J.: Prentice-Hall, 1956/ paperback ed. W. W. Norton, 1965.

Dickinson, Peter. "A Defense of Rubbish," *Children's literature in education*, No. 3. November 1970.

Gardner, Helen. *The Business of Criticism*. Oxford: Oxford University Press, 1959.

Garner, Alan, ed. *The Hamish Hamilton Book of Goblins*. London: Hamish Hamilton, 1969.

Hoggart, Richard. "Teaching Literature to Adults," *About Literature*, vol. 2 of *Speaking to Each Other*. London: Chatto and Windus, 1970/ New York: Oxford University Press, 1970.

Hoggart, Richard. *The Uses of Literacy: Aspects of Working-Class Life, with Special References to Publications & Entertainments*. London: Chatto and Windus, 1957/ paperback ed. New York: Oxford University Press, 1970.

Holman, Felice. *Slake's Limbo*. New York: Charles Scribner's Sons, 1974/ paperback ed. New York: Dell Publishing Co., 1977/ London: The Macmillan Company, 1980.

Holman, Felice. "*Slake's Limbo*: In Which a Book Switches Authors," *The Horn Book Magazine*, October 1976.

Kingman, Lee, and others, eds. *Illustrators of Children's Books: 1967-1976*. Boston: The Horn Book, Inc., 1978.

Kirkpatrick, D. L., ed. *Twentieth-Century Children's Writers*. London: Macmillan Press, Ltd., 1978/New York: St. Martin's Press, 1978.

Lewis, C. S. *An Experiment in Criticism*. Cambridge: Cambridge University Press, 1961.

Mann, Peter H., and Burgoyne, Jacqueline L. *Books and Reading*. London: André Deutsch, 1969.

Meek, Margaret, and others, eds. *The Cool Web: Patterns of Children's Reading*. London: The Bodley Head, 1977/ New York: Atheneum Publishers, 1978.

Moffett, James. *Teaching the Universe of Discourse*. Boston: Houghton Mifflin Company, 1968.

Sayers, Frances Clarke. *Summoned by Books*. New York: The Viking Press, 1965.

Schücking, Levin. *The Sociology of Literary Taste*. 2nd ed. London: Routledge and Kegan Paul, 1966/ paperback ed., Chicago: University of Chicago Press, 1974.

Stott, John. "Criticism and the Teaching of Stories to Children," *Signal* 32, May 1980.

Trilling, Lionel. Introduction to *Huckleberry Finn* by Mark Twain. New York: Rinehart, 1948.

Wain, John. *A House for the Truth: Critical Essays*. New York: The Viking Press, 1973.

Werner, John. *The Practice of English Teaching*. Graham Owens and Michael Marland, eds. London: Blackie, 1970.

Index

Acknowledgments

Page 223 constitutes an extension of the copyright page. Permission to quote from the text of copyrighted works is gratefully acknowledged to the following:

Excerpt from *Language and Learning* by James Britton. Copyright © James Britton, 1970. Reprinted by permission of Penguin Books Ltd.

"The Appreciation of Literature" by Lord David Cecil. © Lord David Cecil 1971. Reprinted by permission of David Higham Associates Limited.

Excerpts from *The Ordinary and the Fabulous* by Elizabeth Cook. © Cambridge University Press 1969. Reprinted by permission of Cambridge University Press.

Excerpt from "A Defense of Rubbish" by Peter Dickinson. © Peter Dickinson 1970. Reprinted by permission of Agathon Press, Inc., from *Children's literature in education* No. 3, 1970.

Excerpt from *The Business of Criticism* by Helen Gardner. © Oxford University Press 1959. Reprinted by permission of Oxford University Press.

Excerpt from "Yallery Brown," *The Hamish Hamilton Book of Goblins*, edited by Alan Garner. © Alan Garner 1969. Reprinted by permission of Hamish Hamilton Limited.

"Why I Value Literature" from *Speaking to Each Other*, Volume 2, by Richard Hoggart. © Richard Hoggart 1970. Reprinted by permission of Chatto and Windus Ltd., London, and Oxford University Press, New York.

Excerpts from *The Uses of Literacy: Aspects of Working Class Life* by Richard Hoggart. © Richard Hoggart 1957. Reprinted by permission of Chatto and Windus Ltd.

Excerpts from *An Experiment in Criticism* by C. S. Lewis. © Cambridge University Press 1961. Reprinted by permission of Cambridge University Press.

Excerpt from *Books and Reading* by Peter H. Mann and Jacqueline Burgoyne. © Peter H. Mann 1969. Reprinted by permission of André Deutsch.

Excerpt from *Teaching the Universe of Discourse* by James Moffett. Houghton Mifflin Company © 1968. Reprinted by permission of the National Council of Teachers of English.

Excerpts from *Summoned by Books* by Frances Clarke Sayers and Marjeanne Blinn. Copyright © 1965 by Frances Clarke Sayers and Marjeanne Blinn. Reprinted by permission of Viking Penguin Inc.

Excerpts from *The Sociology of Literary Taste* by Levin Schücking. Second Edition (revised and reset) © Routledge and Kegan Paul Ltd. 1966. Reprinted by permission of Routledge and Kegan Paul Ltd. and University of Chicago Press.

Excerpts from "Criticism and the Teaching of Stories to Children" by Jon Stott. © Jon C. Stott 1980. Reprinted by kind permission of the author and *Signal*.

Excerpts from *The Practice of English Teaching* by John Werner, edited by Graham Owens and Michael Marland. © Blackie Publishing Group 1970. Reproduced by kind permission of the Blackie Publishing Group, Bishopbriggs, Glasgow.

Acknowledgment is also made to Routledge and Kegan Paul as publisher of *A Dictionary of British Folk Tales*, Volume 2, Katherine M. Briggs, editor, © K. M. Briggs 1971, from which a Westmorland tale in the public domain has been excerpted.